COMMON CORE LANGUAGE ARTS 4 Today

Daily
Skill Practice

Grade 1

Jeanette Moore Ritch

Carson-Dellosa Publishing, LLC
Greensboro, North Carolina

Credits

Content Editor: Jennifer B. Stith
Copy Editor: Julie B. Killian

 Visit *carsondellosa.com* for correlations to Common Core State, national, and Canadian provincial standards.

Carson-Dellosa Publishing, LLC
PO Box 35665
Greensboro, NC 27425 USA
carsondellosa.com

ISBN 978-1-62442-604-9
02-259131151

Table of Contents

Introduction

Common Core Language Arts 4 Today: Daily Skill Practice is a perfect supplement to any classroom language arts curriculum. Students' reading skills will grow as they work on comprehension, fluency, vocabulary, and decoding. Students' writing skills will improve as they work on elements of writing, writing structure, genre, parts of speech, grammar, and spelling, as well as the writing process.

This book covers 40 weeks of daily practice. Included are language arts exercises for four days a week. These exercises will provide students with ample practice in language arts skills. A separate assessment is included for the fifth day of each week.

Various skills and concepts are reinforced throughout the book through activities that align to the Common Core State Standards. To view these standards, please see the Common Core State Standards Alignment Matrix on pages 7 and 8.

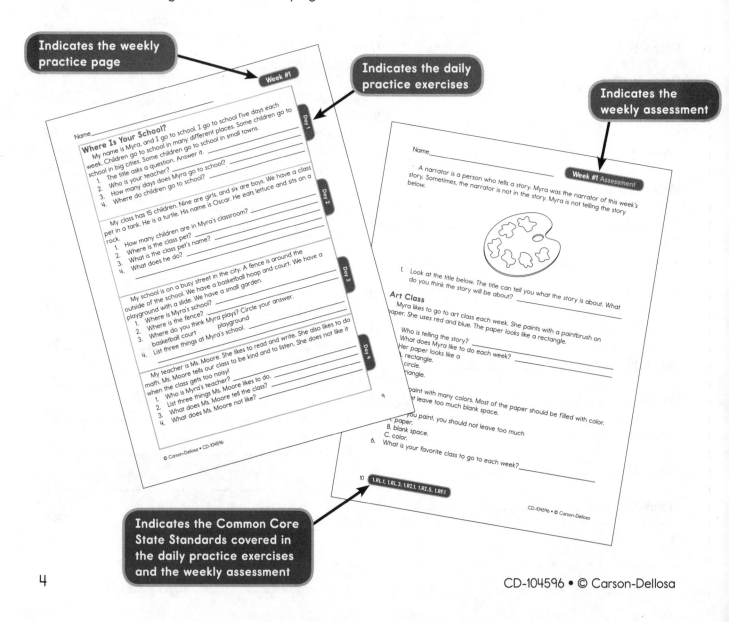

Indicates the weekly practice page

Indicates the daily practice exercises

Indicates the weekly assessment

Indicates the Common Core State Standards covered in the daily practice exercises and the weekly assessment

Building a Reading Environment

A positive reading environment is essential to fostering successful readers. When building a reading environment, think of students' physical, emotional, and cognitive needs.

Physical Environment
- Make the physical reading environment inviting and comfortable. Create a reading corner with comfortable chairs, floor pillows, a rug, enticing lighting, etc.
- Give students access to a variety of texts by providing books, magazines, newspapers, and Internet access. Read signs, ads, posters, menus, pamphlets, labels, boxes, and more!
- Provide regularly scheduled independent reading time in class. Encourage students to read at home. They can read to a younger sibling or read anything of interest such as comic books, children's and sports magazines, chapter books, etc.
- Set a positive example. Make sure students see you reading too!

Emotional Environment
- Learn about students' reading habits, preferences, strengths, and weaknesses. Then, provide books that address these issues.
- Help students create connections with text. Facilitate connections by activating prior knowledge, examining personal meaning, and respecting personal reflections.
- Give students the opportunity to choose titles to read. This will give them a sense of ownership, which will engage them in the text and sustain interest.
- Create a safe environment for exploring and trying new things. Foster a feeling of mutual respect for reading abilities and preferences.
- Require students to read at an appropriate reading level. Text in any content area, including leisure reading, should not be too easy or too difficult.
- Have all students participate in reading, regardless of their reading levels. Try to include slower readers and be sure to give them time to finish before moving on or asking questions.
- Be enthusiastic about reading! Talk about books you love and share your reading experiences and habits. Your attitude about reading is contagious!

Cognitive Environment
- Regardless of the grade level, read aloud to students every day. Reading aloud not only provides a good example but also lets students practice their listening skills.
- Help students build their vocabularies to make their reading more successful. Create word walls, personal word lists, mini-dictionaries, and graphic organizers.
- Read for different purposes. Reading a novel requires different skills than reading an instruction manual. Teach students the strategies needed to comprehend these different texts.
- Encourage students to talk about what and how they read. Use journal writing, literature circles, class discussions, conferences, conversations, workshops, seminars, and more.
- Writing and reading are inherently linked. Students can examine their own writing through reading and examine their reading skills by writing. Whenever possible, facilitate the link between reading and writing.

Choose a **topic** for your writing.
- What am I writing about?

Decide on a **purpose** for writing.
- Why am I writing this piece?
- What do I hope the audience will learn from reading this piece?

Identify your **audience**.
- Who am I writing to?

Decide on a writing **style**.
- Expository—gives information or explains facts or ideas
- Persuasive—tries to talk someone into something
- Narrative—tells a story
- Descriptive—presents a clear picture of a person, place, thing, or idea

Decide on a **genre**—essay, letter, poetry, autobiography, fiction, or nonfiction.

Decide on a **point of view**—first person, second person, or third person.

Brainstorm by listing or drawing your main ideas.

Use a graphic organizer to **organize** your thoughts.

Revise, revise, revise!
- Use **descriptive words**.
- Use **transitions** and linking expressions.
- Use a **variety of sentence structures**.
- **Elaborate** with facts and details.
- Group your ideas into **paragraphs**.
- **Proofread** for capitalization, punctuation, and spelling.

Common Core State Standards Alignment Matrix

STANDARD	W1	W2	W3	W4	W5	W6	W7	W8	W9	W10	W11	W12	W13	W14	W15	W16	W17	W18	W19	W20
1.RL.1	●					●	●		●				●				●		●	
1.RL.2							●		●				●						●	
1.RL.3	●								●				●						●	
1.RL.4			●				●		●				●				●			
1.RL.5					●															
1.RL.6			●								●									
1.RL.7															●		●			
1.RL.9			●																●	
1.RL.10																	●			
1.RI.1	●		●		●						●				●					
1.RI.2											●				●					
1.RI.3											●									
1.RI.4			●																	
1.RI.5	●				●															
1.RI.6											●									
1.RI.7										●										
1.RI.8																				
1.RI.9																				
1.RI.10					●						●									
1.RF.1	●					●									●					
1.RF.2		●				●		●		●		●						●		●
1.RF.3		●				●		●		●		●						●		●
1.RF.4			●		●	●	●				●		●		●					
1.W.1																				
1.W.2									●				●		●					
1.W.3																				
1.W.5			●						●						●					
1.W.6																				
1.W.7															●					
1.W.8			●																●	
1.L.1		●		●		●		●		●		●	●	●	●	●				
1.L.2		●		●		●		●										●		●
1.L.4			●	●										●						
1.L.5			●	●							●			●					●	
1.L.6																●				

W = Week

© Carson-Dellosa • CD-104596   7

STANDARD	W21	W22	W23	W24	W25	W26	W27	W28	W29	W30	W31	W32	W33	W34	W35	W36	W37	W38	W39	W40
1.RL.1			●				●				●		●		●		●		●	
1.RL.2			●				●				●		●		●		●		●	
1.RL.3			●				●				●		●				●			
1.RL.4			●				●						●		●					
1.RL.5															●					
1.RL.6																	●			
1.RL.7																				
1.RL.9											●								●	
1.RL.10					●															
1.RI.1	●				●				●											
1.RI.2	●				●				●											
1.RI.3									●											
1.RI.4																				
1.RI.5																				
1.RI.6																				
1.RI.7	●																			
1.RI.8									●											
1.RI.9	●																			
1.RI.10	●								●											
1.RF.1	●		●															●		
1.RF.2		●												●				●		
1.RF.3		●				●				●				●		●		●		
1.RF.4				●	●	●		●			●		●		●					
1.W.1															●				●	
1.W.2									●											
1.W.3			●				●		●				●		●					
1.W.5													●							
1.W.6															●		●			
1.W.7																				
1.W.8																			●	
1.L.1					●		●		●	●		●								●
1.L.2		●			●		●		●			●		●						●
1.L.4		●			●	●												●		
1.L.5						●					●					●				
1.L.6												●		●						

W = Week

Name_____

Where Is Your School?

My name is Myra, and I go to school. I go to school five days each week. Children go to school in many different places. Some children go to school in big cities. Some children go to school in small towns.

1. The title asks a question. Answer it. _____
2. Who is your teacher? _____
3. How many days does Myra go to school? _____
4. Where do children go to school? _____

Day 1

My class has 15 children. Nine are girls, and six are boys. We have a class pet in a tank. He is a turtle. His name is Oscar. He eats lettuce and sits on a rock.

1. How many children are in Myra's classroom? _____
2. Where is the class pet? _____
3. What is the class pet's name? _____
4. What does he do? _____
_____

Day 2

My school is on a busy street in the city. A fence is around the outside of the school. We have a basketball hoop and court. We have a playground with a slide. We have a small garden.

1. Where is Myra's school? _____
2. Where is the fence? _____
3. Where do you think Myra plays? Circle your answer.
   basketball court   playground
4. List three things at Myra's school. _____
_____

Day 3

My teacher is Ms. Moore. She likes to read and write. She also likes to do math. Ms. Moore tells our class to be kind and to listen. She does not like it when the class gets too noisy!

1. Who is Myra's teacher? _____
2. List three things Ms. Moore likes to do. _____
3. What does Ms. Moore tell the class? _____
4. What does Ms. Moore not like? _____

Day 4

A narrator is a person who tells a story. Myra was the narrator of this week's story. Sometimes, the narrator is not in the story. Myra is not telling the story below.

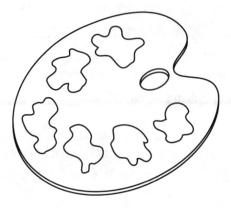

1. Look at the title below. The title can tell you what the story is about. What do you think the story will be about? _____

Art Class

Myra likes to go to art class each week. She paints with a paintbrush on paper. She uses red and blue. The paper looks like a rectangle.

2. Who is telling the story? _____
3. What does Myra like to do each week? _____
4. Her paper looks like a
   A. rectangle.
   B. circle.
   C. triangle.

You can paint with many colors. Most of the paper should be filled with color. You should not leave too much blank space.

5. When you paint, you should not leave too much
   A. paper.
   B. blank space.
   C. color.
6. What is your favorite class to go to each week?_____

Name_____

1. A sentence starts with a capital letter. Use a capital letter.
   (my) _____ dog takes a bath.
2. Circle the picture whose name has the **short a** sound.
3. Put a period at the end of a sentence that tells something.
   The dog and the cat have fur
4. Circle the correct words.   cit or cat ?   buth or bath ?

1. Use a capital letter.
   (we) _____ go to the park.
2. Circle the picture whose name has the **short i** sound.
3. Put a period at the end of a sentence that tells something.
   The fish like to swim
4. Circle the correct words.   fish or fash ?   swom or swim ?

1. Use a capital letter.
   (jake) _____ sees the pond.
2. Circle the picture whose name has the **short o** sound.
3. Put a period at the end of a sentence that tells something.
   The mop is wet
4. Circle the correct words.   pind or pond ?   mop or mup ?

1. Use a capital letter.
   (the) _____ boy likes to run.
2. Circle the picture whose name has the **short u** sound.

3. Put a period at the end of a sentence that tells something.
   The boy jumps up
4. Circle the correct words.   ap or up ?   rin or run ?

Name_____

Write the first word of each sentence. Use a capital letter.

1. (kit) _____ will go to the store.

2. (please) _____ look at the map.

3. (they) _____ will play.

Circle the pictures whose names have short vowel sounds.

4.

5.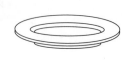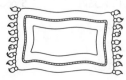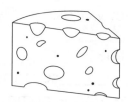

Read each sentence. Put a period at the end if the sentence tells something. Put a question mark at the end if the sentence asks a question.

6. Where are you going

7. I see a red truck

8. Lee is in the car

Circle each correct word.

9. nap or nop ?

10. rug or rog ?

1.RF.2, 1.RF.3, 1.L.1, 1.L.2

Name_____

Shadow Play

Can you see your shadow? You can play with shadows. You can use your hands to make shapes on a wall. Shadows move when you move.

1. What can you do with shadows? _____

2. What can you do with your hands? _____
_____

3. Write a sentence about a time you saw a shadow. What did it look like? _____
_____

You can see a shadow when light is on one side of you. The light makes the shadow. The shadow is on the other side. When you are inside, lamps and flashlights make shadows. When you are outside, the sun makes shadows.

1. What makes shadows when you are inside? _____

2. What makes shadows when you are outside?_____

3. Write a sentence about how a shadow is made. _____
_____

Do you see a shadow in front of you? If you do, then the light is behind you. Is your shadow behind you? Then, the light is in front of you. Shadows are dark, but they are made by light.

1. Where is the light if the shadow is in front of you? _____

2. Where is the light if the shadow is behind you?_____
_____

3. Write a sentence about a time you stepped on a shadow. What happened?_____
_____

Shadow play is fun. You can move your hands to show pictures. You can even show animals. Some animals you can make are farm animals such as ducks. You can make alligators and rabbits too.

1. What kind of shadows can you make with your hands? _____
_____

2. Name three animals you can make. _____

3. Write a sentence about a shadow play you could make with a friend.
_____
_____

A play is when people get together and pretend. People who pretend are actors. They can tell a story. Plays have more than one person who talks. The actors can also dance, play, and move. Some actors sing in plays.

Read the play by yourself or with a friend.

Did You See That?

Rosa: Hi, Jared. I am so glad you came to the tree house.

Jared: I am glad too. Are you OK?

Rosa: I was scared.

Jared: Why were you scared?

Rosa: It is dark in the tree house today. I thought I saw something.

Jared: Do not worry, Rosa. Nothing is in the tree house.

Rosa: Look behind you!

Jared: What? I do not see anything.

Rosa: I thought I saw a dark spot!

Jared: Oh, Rosa. That is just my shadow!

Rosa: Silly me!

1. What happened first?
   A. Jared came to the tree house.
   B. Rosa saw Jared's shadow.
   C. Rosa told Jared the tree house was dark.

2. What happened second?
   A. Jared came to the tree house.
   B. Rosa saw Jared's shadow.
   C. Rosa told Jared the tree house was dark.

3. What happened third?
   A. Jared came to the tree house.
   B. Rosa saw Jared's shadow.
   C. Rosa told Jared the tree house was dark.

4. Where do you see shadows? Write a sentence. _____

_____

A noun is a person, a place, a thing, or an idea. Write three nouns.

_____   _____   _____

Some plural nouns have **-s** on the end. It means there is more than one.
   Example: dog   dogs

Make each noun plural by adding **-s** to the end.

animal___   bear___   boy___   girl___

Day 1

Write three nouns.

_____   _____   _____

Make each noun plural by adding **-s** to the end.

top___   number___   lake___   car___

Day 2

Write three nouns.

_____   _____   _____

Make each noun plural by adding **-s** to the end.

wig___   horse___   face___   lid___

Day 3

Write three nouns.

_____   _____   _____

Make each noun plural by adding **-s** to the end.

clam___   key___   bat___   jet___

Day 4

1. Circle the five nouns.

    said   with   hat   kick   pup   bib   write   can   bag   sweep

2. Draw one noun from above.

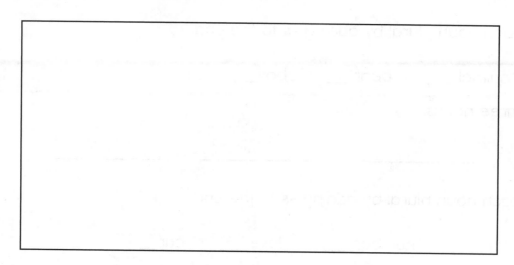

3. Write a sentence about the picture above.

    _____

    _____

4. Look at question 1 again. Make each noun plural by adding **-s** to the end.

    _____

    _____

    _____

    _____

    _____

5. Write a sentence using one of the plural nouns from question 4.

    _____

    _____

1.L.1, 1.L.2, 1.L.4, 1.L.5   CD-104596 • © Carson-Dellosa

Name_____

Rice Is Nice

Rice is a food. Many people in the world eat rice a few times a day. Almost all rice is grown in ponds. The rice crops need a lot of rain to grow.

1. Who eats rice? _____
2. Where is rice grown? _____
3. What do rice crops need? _____
4. Write a sentence about a time you ate rice. _____
_____

Rice grows in thick mud. It looks like grass. At first, the rice stands tall. When the rice is ready to be picked, it bends.

1. Where does rice grow? _____
2. What does it look like? _____
3. What happens to rice when it is ready to be picked? _____
_____
4. Draw a picture of the rice plant.

A rice field is large with patches. The patches look like holes in the field. These patches are easy to fill with water. New seeds are planted in the holes with a tool. Some seeds are even dropped from a small airplane.

1. What does a rice field look like?_____
2. What do patches look like? _____
3. What are seeds planted with? _____
4. What do you think about seeds dropping from an airplane? Write a sentence about it. _____
_____

Rice is used to feed people and animals. Hats, bags, and rope are made from rice straw. Rice can be put on plants to help them grow. It can be used in medicine. Rice is very useful!

1. What is made with rice straw? _____
2. What can rice do to plants? _____
3. What can rice be used in? _____
4. Rice can be eaten with other foods such as chicken. Write a sentence about your favorite rice dish. _____
_____

True or False?

Some text gives you new information. Each piece of new information is called a fact. A fact is true. You can find facts in the dictionary, in books, and on the Internet.

Read each sentence. Circle **True** if it is a fact. Circle **False** if it is not a fact.

1. Dogs have ears.
   True   False

2. Rain is wet.
   True   False

3. The beach does not have sand.
   True   False

4. A bike has wheels.
   True   False

5. All cats have blue eyes.
   True   False

6. The word **ball** starts with the letter **r**.
   True   False

7. Books do not have pages.
   True   False

8. Plants need the sun to grow.
   True   False

9. Butterflies cannot fly.
   True   False

10. Snow is warm.
    True   False

1.RL.5, 1.RI.1, 1.RI.5, 1.RI.10, 1.RF.4

Name_____

A proper noun starts with a capital letter. A proper noun is the name of a person, a place, or a thing. Capitalize each proper noun.

paul _____   norwalk _____

kit _____   washington _____

Most words that end with **-e** have a long vowel. The long vowel says its name. Add **-e** to turn each short vowel word into a long vowel word.

tap__   mop__   cap__   ton__

Capitalize each proper noun.

pascal _____   virginia _____

walsh _____   utah _____

Add **-e** to turn each short vowel word into a long vowel word.

rip__   pin__   dim__   bit__

Capitalize each proper noun.

lewis _____   scottsville _____

mario _____   california _____

Add **-e** to turn each short vowel word into a long vowel word.

fin__   tub__   hid__   cut__

Capitalize each proper noun.

ross _____   montana _____

yvette _____   newburgh _____

Add **-e** to turn each short vowel word into a long vowel word.

rat__   cub__   shin__   gap__

1. Read the story. Find and circle 10 proper nouns.

Snowfall

Matt wanted it to snow. He looked through the window. He did not see any snow yet. He saw his dog.

"Rider! Come here, pup," Matt said.

Rider did not hear Matt. Matt went outside to get him. Matt called for him again. His brother came to help.

"Thanks for your help, Darius," Matt said.

They saw Rider. He was barking at the sky. The snow was falling!

2. Which three names did you circle?

   _____

   _____

   _____

3. Why are they proper nouns?

   _____

   _____

4. Circle the five pictures whose names have short vowel sounds.

5. Circle the five pictures whose names have long vowel sounds.

1.RL.1, 1.RF.1, 1.RF.2, 1.RF.3, 1.RF.4, 1.L.1, 1.L.2

Sharks

Sharks live in the ocean. They have been here for thousands of years. In the ocean are more than 350 kinds of sharks. Some sharks have big teeth. Others have small teeth.

1. Where do sharks live? _____
2. How long have they been here? _____
3. How many kinds of sharks are there? _____
4. What are sharks' teeth like? _____

Day 1

Sharks have to open their mouths so that they can breathe. They keep their mouths open when they swim. We can see their teeth! It may look scary, but they are just breathing.

1. How do sharks breathe? _____
2. Why are their mouths open when they swim? _____
3. What do you see if a shark's mouth is open? _____
4. How do you feel when you see sharp teeth? Write a sentence.

_____

_____

Day 2

Sharks can be long or short. Some sharks can grow to be up to 36 feet long! Other sharks are only six inches long. That is the length of a stapler. Some sharks are small enough to live in small fish tanks. Large sharks can be at an aquarium and live in large fish tanks.

1. How big are sharks? _____
2. What object is about six inches long? _____
3. Which sharks live in fish tanks? _____
4. Which sharks live in aquariums? _____

Day 3

Many people hunt sharks. A shark can get caught in a net. Shark skin can be used for belts. Some people eat shark meat. Others eat shark fin soup.

1. What is shark skin used for? _____
2. What do people eat from the shark? _____
3. Where do sharks get caught? _____
4. What do you think shark fin soup tastes like? Write a sentence.

_____

_____

Day 4

Question words are important. They help you find information.

    Who or What?
    Where?
    When?
    Why?
    How?

Read the story.

Mugu Moja

    A chimpanzee was caught in a trap in 2007. She was very young. Her name was Mugu Moja. She lived in Africa. The trap was around her leg. A man took the trap off of her. Her leg was hurt. A doctor took care of her.

    Mugu Moja taught people a lesson. Men and women now know that some traps in Africa catch chimps. Men and women can save chimps like Mugu Moja. She lives in the jungle now and is very happy. No more traps are in her jungle.

1.   Who is the main topic of the story? _____

2.   What type of animal is she? _____

3.   Where does she live? _____

4.   When was she trapped? _____

5.   What lesson did she teach? _____

6.   How does she feel now? _____

Some verbs are action words. They show movement. Circle each verb.
1. Yosef rides his bike.
2. Claire holds the fork.
3. Mia smells the food.
4. Taylor sees her mom.

Blends are two or more letters that make sounds together. They can start words. Circle the blend in each word.

5. blue
6. blip
7. blot
8. blur

Circle each verb.
1. Cara calls for her dad.
2. Eric looks outside.
3. Jessi sits in her seat.
4. Victor plays ball.

Circle the blend in each word.

5. fry
6. frown
7. from
8. frog

Circle each verb.
1. Kevin runs to school.
2. Zach jumps rope.
3. Vanessa finds her doll.
4. Molly lifts the blinds.

Circle the blend in each word.

5. try
6. trip
7. trike
8. true

Circle each verb.
1. Rusty makes cookies.
2. Jeff sells apples.
3. Nora cleans her room.
4. Mariah swims in the pool.

Circle the blend in each word.

5. stay
6. steel
7. still
8. stuff

Some verbs show action. Some verbs show movement.

1. This is a verb web. Write verbs on the lines.

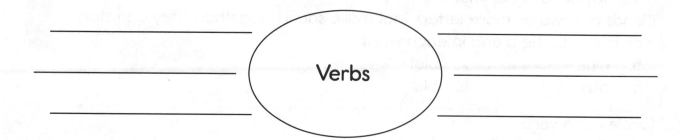

2. Write two sentences. Each one should have a verb.
    A.
    _____
    _____

    B.
    _____
    _____

A blend is two or more letters that make sounds together. Blends can start words.

3. Write a word that starts with each blend. The first one has been done for you.

    br **ick**   dr _____

    cl _____   cr _____

    gr _____   fl _____

    gl _____   sl _____

1.RF.2, 1.RF.3, 1.L.1, 1.L.2

A Wish Come True

Liv wanted to do one thing. She wanted to ride a horse. She loved horses. She read horse books at the library. She drew horses in art class. She had horse pictures in her room.

1. What did Liv want to do? _____
2. What kind of books did she read at the library? _____
3. Where did she draw horses? _____
4. How do you know she loves horses? Write a sentence. _____
_____

Day 1

One day, Liv got what she wanted. Liv's aunt knew a woman who had a horse farm. Liv's aunt took her to the horse farm. Liv saw two horses. Liv liked Henry the best. Henry had brown fur. His eyes were round and black.

1. Who took Liv to the horse farm?_____
2. How many horses did Liv see? _____
3. Which horse was Liv's favorite? _____
4. Write a sentence to describe Henry. _____
_____

Day 2

Liv loved being with Henry. She pet his mane. It felt soft in her hands. She asked the woman if she could feed Henry. The woman said yes! They walked to the stable to get a carrot. Liv fed one to Henry. He ate fast!

1. How did Henry's mane feel? _____
2. What did Liv ask the woman? _____
3. Where was the carrot? _____
4. How do you know that Henry was hungry? _____
_____

Day 3

Liv liked Henry. The woman spoke to Liv's aunt. She said Liv could sit on Henry. Liv jumped up and down! She had never sat on a horse before. Liv placed a helmet on her head. She smiled. The woman put Liv on Henry's back.

1. What did the woman tell Liv's aunt? _____
2. What did Liv do? _____
3. What did Liv place on her head? _____
4. How did Liv feel when she sat on Henry? Write a sentence. _____
_____

Day 4

What Do You Want to Do?

Children want to do many things. Some children want to go fishing or bike riding. Others want to go to a store or a restaurant. Children want to travel or visit a friend. Boys and girls like to do different things.

1. What do you want to do? Write a sentence. _____

_____

2. Draw a picture of what you want to do.

```

```

3. Write about what you want to do. Complete each sentence.

First sentence: I want to _____.

Detail sentence: I have wanted to do this since _____.

Detail sentence: I want to do this because _____.

Detail sentence: When I _____, I will feel _____.

Last sentence: I cannot wait to _____!

1. Adjectives are describing words. Circle the picture that matches the adjective.

   hot

2. Write a word to describe a ball. _____

3. **Ay** is a vowel team. It makes the **/ā/** sound.
   What rhymes with **day**? _____ _____ _____
   Circle each **ay** vowel team.   May   play   okay   Ray

Day 1

1. Circle the picture that matches the adjective.

   cold

2. Write a word to describe a flower. _____

3. **Ai** is a vowel team. It makes the **/ā/** sound.
   What rhymes with **pail**? _____ _____ _____
   Circle each **ai** vowel team.   snail   trait   Kait   main

Day 2

1. Circle the picture that matches the adjective.

   soft

2. Write a word to describe a slide. _____

3. **Ea** is a vowel team. It makes the **/ē/** sound.
   What rhymes with **meat**? _____ _____ _____
   Circle each **ea** vowel team.   each   squeal   pea   leave

Day 3

1. Circle the picture that matches the adjective.

   fast

2. Write a word to describe a box. _____

3. **Ee** is a vowel team. It makes the **/ē/** sound.
   What rhymes with **glee**? _____ _____ _____
   Circle each **ee** vowel team.   peel   wheel   eel   see

Day 4

Name_____

Adjectives help you describe things. You can use your five senses:

sight
smell
touch
hearing
taste

Use a word from the box to complete each sentence.

1. The sky is _____.

2. The cat is _____.

3. The tree is _____.

4. The sock is _____.

5. The food is _____.

| stinky |
| tall |
| furry |
| blue |
| hot |

Look at the picture. Write five things you see. The first sentence has been started for you.

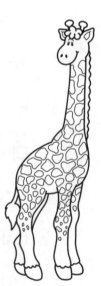

6. The giraffe has a _____ neck.

7. _____

8. _____

9. _____

10. _____

1.RI.7, 1.RF.2, 1.RF.3, 1.L.1   CD-104596 • © Carson-Dellosa

A Large Bird

The ostrich is a large bird. It has long legs and a long neck. It has a large body. An ostrich can grow to be up to nine feet tall. It is taller than a man. It is so big that it cannot fly.

1. What is an ostrich? _____
2. How tall can an ostrich grow? _____
3. What is an ostrich taller than? _____
4. Why can an ostrich not fly? Write a sentence. _____
_____

Day 1

An ostrich cannot fly, but it can run. Its long legs are very strong. One ostrich step can cover up to 16 feet! That is almost as long as a car. This bird can also run fast because of its strong legs. It keeps balance with its short wings.

1. What can an ostrich do? _____
2. How long is an ostrich step? _____
3. Why does an ostrich run fast? _____
4. How does it keep its balance? Write a sentence. _____
_____

Day 2

Most birds have four toes. The ostrich only has two toes. It is the only bird with two toes. It also has a claw that is four inches long. The two toes and the claw help the ostrich dig into the dirt as it runs to get speed.

1. How many toes do most birds have? _____
2. How many toes does the ostrich have? _____
3. How long are the ostrich's claws? _____
4. What helps the ostrich run? Write a sentence. _____
_____

Day 3

The ostrich lays the largest eggs of all birds. It hides its eggs in the sand. Male and female ostriches take care of the eggs. A nest can have up to 60 eggs! These eggs take 40 days to hatch. That is about five weeks.

1. Where does the ostrich hide eggs? _____
2. Who takes care of the eggs? _____
3. How many eggs are in a nest? _____
4. How long does it take the eggs to hatch? Write a sentence. _____
_____

Day 4

Animal Families

Animals are part of families. The ostrich is part of the bird family. Many kinds of birds are in the bird family. They all have wings and beaks. They lay eggs.

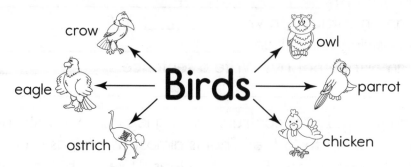

1. Cats are part of the feline family. Circle the three members of the feline family.

2. What do the feline family members share? Write two sentences.

    _____

    _____

3. Dogs are part of the canine family. Circle the three members of the canine family.

4. What do the canine family members share? Write two sentences.

    _____

    _____

1.RL.6, 1.RI.1, 1.RI.2, 1.RI.3, 1.RI.6, 1.RI.10, 1.RF.4, 1.L.5

A contraction is two words that become one. A contraction has an apostrophe.

1. is not = isn't   What letter is replaced by the apostrophe? _____
2. do not = _____

The letters **ow** can sound like the **/ow/** in **now**.

3. **Now** rhymes with _____, _____, and _____.
4. Circle the two pictures whose names have the **/ow/** sound.

A contraction is two words that become one. A contraction has an apostrophe.

1. you are = you're   What letter is replaced by the apostrophe? _____
2. we are = _____

The letters **ow** can sound like the **/ō/** in **snow**.

3. **Snow** rhymes with _____, _____, and _____.
4. Circle the two pictures whose names have the **/ō/** sound.

A contraction is two words that become one. A contraction has an apostrophe.

1. has not = hasn't What letter is replaced by the apostrophe? _____
2. had not = _____

The letter **y** can sound like the **y** in **fry**. It sounds like **/ī/**.

3. **Fry** rhymes with _____, _____, and _____.
4. Circle the one picture whose name has the the **/ī/** sound.

A contraction is two words that become one. A contraction has an apostrophe.

1. he is = he's   What letter is replaced by the apostrophe? _____
2. she is = _____

The letter **y** can sound like the **y** in **berry**. It sounds like **/ē/**.

3. **Berry** rhymes with _____, _____, and _____.
4. Circle the one picture whose name has the **/ē/** sound.

A contraction is two words that become one word. They lose a letter. Sometimes, they lose two letters.

Write a sentence or a question for each contraction. Look at the end of the line for a clue.

1. She's _____.

2. You're _____.

3. Isn't _____?

4. Don't _____?

5. I'm _____.

Sort the words by their sounds.

blow	why
my	foggy
carry	flow
towel	tower

/ow/ as in **now**   **/ō/** as in **snow**   **/ī/** as in **fry**   **/ē/** as in **berry**

_____   _____   _____   _____

_____   _____   _____   _____

Fun Onstage

Ming went to see a play with her grandmother. Ming saw actors on the stage. They looked like they were having fun. When Ming went onstage at school, she felt bad. She felt dizzy. She wanted to have fun like the actors.

1. Whom did Ming go to the play with? _____
2. What did Ming see? _____
3. What happened when Ming went onstage at school? _____
4. How did Ming feel? Write a sentence. _____
   _____

Day 1

Ming liked to watch the actors. They knew how to say their lines. They moved onstage. They danced and sang. Ming wanted to have fun like they do. She needed someone to help her.

1. Whom did Ming like to watch? _____
2. What did the actors do? _____
3. What did Ming want? _____
4. What did Ming need? Write a sentence. _____
   _____

Day 2

Ming asked her grandmother a question. She asked if she could have a teacher to help her learn to act. Ming wanted to learn how to have fun onstage. Her grandmother said it was a good idea. Her grandmother called an acting teacher. Ming was happy!

1. What did Ming ask her grandmother? _____
2. What does Ming want to learn? _____
3. What did Ming's grandmother do? _____
4. How did Ming feel? Write a sentence. _____
   _____

Day 3

Ming met Mr. Walker. Mr. Walker has been an acting teacher for 10 years. He was an actor when he was young. He likes to help children learn to act onstage. Ming had her first lesson with Mr. Walker. She felt calm now. She was brave. She was ready for the stage!

1. Who is Mr. Walker? _____
2. What was Mr. Walker when he was young? _____
3. What did Mr. Walker like to do? _____
4. How did Ming feel after her first lesson? Write a sentence. _____
   _____

Day 4

Give It a Try!

Trying a new sport or activity can be scary. Some kids feel nervous or worried. They might feel "butterflies in their stomachs." But, it is good to try new things. It is good to be brave and to try your best.

1. Did you ever want to try something new? Write a sentence.

_____

_____

2. Did you try it? How did you feel? Write a sentence.

_____

_____

3. When did you feel better? Write a sentence.

_____

_____

4. What would you tell a friend who wanted to try this? Write three sentences of advice to help your friend feel stronger.
A.

_____

_____

B.

_____

_____

C.

_____

_____

1.RL.1, 1.RL.2, 1.RL.3, 1.RL.4, 1.RF.4, 1.W.2, 1.L.1

Some words are strong adjectives. Make each adjective stronger.
1. big = HUGE
    small = _____

Some words have more than one meaning.
2. ring – on a finger
    ring – _____

Make each adjective stronger.
1. warm = HOT
    cold = _____

Some words have more than one meaning.
2. watch – to look
    watch – _____

Make each adjective stronger.
1. soft = FLUFFY
    large = _____

Some words have more than one meaning.
2. can – to be able to do something
    can – _____

Make each adjective stronger.
1. look = STARE
    talk = _____

Some words have more than one meaning.
2. mouse – computer part or tool
    mouse – _____

Stronger Words

Adjectives are words that describe things. Some adjectives are strong. They replace regular adjectives.

1. Draw a line to match each adjective to the stronger adjective.

big	tiny
small	giant
hot	icy
cold	boiling

Some words have more than one meaning.

2. bark – part of a tree
   bark – _____

3. bat – used in baseball
   bat – _____

4. box – a sport
   box – _____

5. clip – put together
   clip – _____

6. club – a big tool or a bat
   club – _____

Name_____

Week #15

Making Maple Syrup

Maple syrup is sold in bottles at grocery stores. It tastes sweet. It is very sticky. It comes from trees. Maple trees have sap that comes out of them. First, the trees need to have holes drilled into them. Then, the sap drips out of the holes.

1. What is the sap like? _____
2. Where does the sap come from? _____
3. What is done first to get the sap? _____
4. What do you pour maple syrup on? _____

Day 1

Maple trees are filled with sweet sap. To get to the sap, holes are drilled into the trees. The second step is to hang a bucket on each tree. The sap falls into the buckets. When it falls into the buckets, it makes a *ping, ping* sound. The buckets are made of metal. The buckets are full at the end of the day.

1. Where does the sap drip from? _____
2. What is the second step? _____
3. What is the bucket made of? _____
4. When is the bucket full? _____

Day 2

At the end of the day, the bucket of sap is taken inside. The sap is kept cool. After a week, it is ready to turn from sap to syrup. The third step is to boil the sap. It is poured into a pot. The pot is placed over a fire in a maple sugaring house. The sap turns a dark color. It must boil for 30 hours to become maple syrup.

1. Where is the bucket of sap taken? _____
2. What is the third step? _____
3. Where is the pot placed? _____
4. What happens to the sap? _____

Day 3

The fire is turned off when the sap turns into syrup. The syrup is poured out of the pots. The fourth step is to pour the syrup into bottles. These bottles of syrup are then sold in stores. This is the yummy syrup we eat!

1. When is the fire turned off? _____
2. What is the fourth step? _____
3. Where are bottles of syrup sold? _____
4. Have you ever tasted maple syrup? Write a sentence. _____
    _____

Day 4

Four Steps

When you want to tell how to do something, you can write steps. When you follow steps, you can reach your goal. In writing, you can use words that show your steps.

first
second
third
fourth

first
then
next
last

Let's Make a Sandwich

Draw a sandwich. Start with bread. Use whatever fillings you like. You can use turkey, lettuce, vegetables, or cheese.

1. First, I get a piece of _____. It is on the bottom.

2. Then, _____.

3. Next, _____.

4. Last, I put another piece of _____ on top.

5. Write a sentence about how your sandwich tastes.

   _____

   _____

1.RL.7, 1.RI.1, 1.RI.2, 1.RF.1, 1.RF.4, 1.W.2, 1.W.5, 1.W.7, 1.L.1

A conjunction joins two words, phrases, or sentences.
Example: We went to the pond and saw the ducks.
The conjunction is **and**. Write a sentence with **and**.
_____

A verb is an action word. It can be in the past, present, or future tense.
     Example:
     Past: played   Present: play   Future: will play
 1. Past: kicked   Present: _____   Future: _____ _____
 2. Past: baked   Present: _____   Future: _____ _____

Day 1

Kevin wanted to play baseball, but he lost his bat.
The conjunction is **but**. Write a sentence with **but**.
_____

A verb is an action word. It can be in the past, present, or future tense.

 1. Past: wanted   Present: _____   Future: _____ _____

 2. Past: laughed   Present: _____   Future: _____ _____

Day 2

He could go to the game, or he could go to the fair.
The conjunction is **or**. Write a sentence with **or**.
_____

A verb is an action word. It can be in the past, present, or future tense.

 1. Past: asked   Present: _____   Future: _____ _____

 2. Past: worked   Present: _____   Future: _____ _____

Day 3

Lauren was inside, so she stayed warm.
The conjunction is **so**. Write a sentence with **so**.
_____

A verb is an action word. It can be in the past, present, or future tense.

 1. Past: lifted   Present: _____   Future: _____ _____

 2. Past: joked   Present: _____   Future: _____ _____

Day 4

Stretching Sentences

A conjunction joins two words, phrases, or sentences. Use the words in the box to complete the sentences.

and	but	or	so

1. Casey found a penny _____ put it in her pocket.

2. Hector wanted to wear shorts, _____ it was snowing.

3. Julia will go to bed now, _____ it is time to turn off her light.

4. Uncle Tad can take me to the zoo, _____ he can take me to the park.

Verbs Tell Time

A verb can be in the past, present, or future tense.
Circle the verb in each sentence. Write if it is **past**, **present**, or **future** tense.

5. Eddie will take a bat. _____

6. The man throws the ball. _____

7. Eddie swings his bat. _____

8. The ball will fly up. _____

9. Eddie hopped on home plate. _____

10. He scored a run! _____

Haiku 5-7-5

Haiku are short poems. Haiku are from Japan. They are about nature. A haiku has 17 syllables. It has three lines. The first line has five syllables. The second line has seven syllables. The third line has five syllables.

1. Where are haiku from? _____

2. What are they about? _____

3. How many syllables are in a haiku? _____

4. How many lines are in a haiku? _____

A haiku is about nature. It has a kigo. Kigo is a Japanese word. It is a season. A haiku is set in spring, summer, autumn, or winter. The kigo of snow means wintertime.

1. What does a haiku poem have? _____

2. What is a **kigo**? _____

3. What are the four seasons?_____

4. What does the kigo of snow mean? _____

Animals are in nature. Some haiku are about animals. Many haiku poems are about seasons. A haiku does not rhyme. This makes it different from other poems. It follows the syllable pattern.

1. What can haiku be about?_____

2. What makes a haiku different?_____

3. What does the poem follow? _____

4. How many syllables are in the word **October**? _____

Long, green, slimy legs,
Jumping on hot lily pads,
Fresh grass and wet mud.

1. What is the animal in the poem? _____

2. What is the season in the poem? _____

3. What words tell the season? _____

4. What is the syllable pattern? _____

Day 1

Day 2

Day 3

Day 4

Nature Poems

Write a haiku. It can be about nature. It can be about an animal. It can be about both.

Line 1: five syllables

_____

Line 2: seven syllables

_____

Line 3: five syllables

_____

Answer each question.

1. What is your haiku about? _____

_____

2. What is the season? _____

3. Draw a picture of your haiku.

Name_____

An exclamatory sentence shows a lot of feeling. Add an exclamation point to the end of each sentence.

1. That is great ___
2. I am happy for you ___
3. This is wild ___

A compound word is two words stuck together. They make one word. Write each compound word.

4. back + pack = _____
5. sun + shine = _____

Add an exclamation point to the end of each sentence.

1. You are the best ___
2. Kayla will win ___
3. That was close ___

Write each compound word.

4. rain + bow = _____
5. eye + ball = _____

Add an exclamation point to the end of each sentence.

1. He did a nice job ___
2. Ivy made the goal ___
3. We had a great party ___

Write each compound word.

4. rain + coat = _____
5. dog + house = _____

Add an exclamation point to the end of each sentence.

1. Watch out ___
2. Abe is running fast___
3. This is fun ___

Write each compound word.

4. sleep + walk = _____
5. life + guard = _____

Name_____

Write three sentences with feeling. Put an exclamation point at the end of each sentence.

Example: We laughed so hard!

1. _____

2. _____

3. _____

Draw lines to match the words to make compound words.

grass   noon

school   board

skate   hopper

after   out

with   house

Write the words.

4. _____

5. _____

6. _____

7. _____

8. _____

1.RF.2, 1.RF.3, 1.L.2   CD-104596 • © Carson-Dellosa

Grandma Kate

Grandma Kate moved into our house last month. She needed us to help her. She has a cane. It helps her walk. She has glasses. They help her see. She has a hearing aid. It helps her hear.

1. Why did Grandma Kate move in? _____
2. How does her cane help? _____
3. How do her glasses help? _____
4. How does her hearing aid help? _____

Grandma Kate has a hearing aid. Sometimes, it does not work. She does not always answer when I ask her something. Sometimes, she does not hear me. Mom says I have to speak up. I talk a little louder. It helps Grandma Kate hear me.

1. What does not always work? _____
2. What does Mom say? _____
3. What helps Grandma Kate hear? _____
4. Do you have a grandmother? Write a sentence about her. _____
_____

I came home from school. Something smelled good in the kitchen. My family sat at the table. We ate dinner. Then, Grandma Kate got up. She walked to the oven. She had a cherry pie. I had a piece. It was tasty!

1. Where did the smell come from? _____
2. Who sat at the table? _____
3. What was in the oven? _____
4. Do you like pie? Write a sentence. _____
_____

Today, Grandma Kate and I will bake. I want to learn to make pie. Grandma Kate will let me mix with a spoon. She wants to make blueberry pie. We have flour and water. We also need eggs and sugar. It will taste great.

1. What will they do? _____
2. What will the child mix with? _____
3. What kind of pie will they make? _____
4. What are four things they need? _____

Name_____

Family is important. Do you love someone in your family? Write the names of some people you love. They can be friends or family. They can even be pets!

_____   I love...   _____

_____   _____

Write three sentences about someone you love. Tell how you feel. Tell what you like about the person or the pet.

1. _____

   _____

2. _____

   _____

3. _____

   _____

46   1.RL.1, 1.RL.2, 1.RL.3, 1.RL.9, 1.W.8, 1.L.5

Name_____

A blend is two consonants that appear together. A blend can be at the end of a word. Circle each ending blend. Write a word that rhymes.

1. bump
   It rhymes with _____.
2. camp
   It rhymes with _____.

Oa is a vowel team. It makes the **/ō/** sound. Circle the **oa** vowel teams.
    boat   float   oat   goal

Circle each ending blend. Write a word that rhymes.

1. land
   It rhymes with _____.
2. sound
   It rhymes with _____.

Oe is a vowel team. It makes the **/ō/** sound. Circle the **oe** vowel teams.
    oboe   Joe   toe   doe

Circle each ending blend. Write a word that rhymes.

1. bank
   It rhymes with _____.
2. sink
   It rhymes with _____.

Ie is a vowel team. It makes the **/ī/** sound. Circle the **ie** vowel teams.
    lie   flies   tie   pie

Circle each ending blend. Write a word that rhymes.

1. fast
   It rhymes with _____.
2. rust
   It rhymes with _____.

Uy is a vowel team. It makes the **/ī/** sound. Circle the **uy** vowel teams.
    buy   guy

Blends

A blend is two or more consonants that appear together in a word. A blend can be at the beginning of a word. A blend can also be at the end of a word.

1. Circle the blend at the beginning of each word.

   plan   shoe   flip

2. Write two new words that have beginning blends.

   _____

   _____

3. Circle the blend at the end of each word.

   paint   tent   limp

4. Write two new words that have ending blends.

   _____

   _____

Vowel Team Fishing

5. Catch the fish whose pictures' names have the /ō/ sound. Write the words on the lines.

   _____

   _____

   _____

   _____

Ladybugs

Ladybugs are in many places. There are about 5,000 types! Most are red with black spots. Farmers love ladybugs. Ladybugs eat pests on farm crops.

1. Where are ladybugs? _____
2. How many types are there? _____
3. What do they look like? _____
4. Why do farmers love ladybugs? _____

Day 1

Ladybugs have six legs. Their bodies look like shells. Ladybugs are bright. Birds eat ladybugs. A ladybug can play dead. This makes birds go away.

1. How many legs does a ladybug have? _____
2. What does a ladybug's body look like? _____
3. What eats ladybugs? _____
4. How does a ladybug make a bird go away? _____

Day 2

A ladybug lays eggs on a leaf. Babies are born in a few days. They are called larvae. They grow fast. Then, they shed their skin. Next, they attach to leaves. Finally, they turn into ladybugs.

1. Where do ladybugs lay eggs? _____
2. What are the babies called at first? _____
3. What do they shed? _____
4. Where are they when they become ladybugs? _____

Day 3

Ladybugs are from Europe. They came to America more than 100 years ago. Ladybugs live in many different places. They like forests. Ladybugs do not like the cold. Ladybugs hide in warm places in winter. They rest under rocks and logs.

1. Where are ladybugs from? _____
2. When did they come to America? _____
3. Where do ladybugs like to live? _____
4. What happens when it gets cold? _____

Day 4

Name_____

Creepy Crawly

Insects are bugs. Some bugs are alike. Some are different. Look at the table. Write an *X* in the box if the bug has wings. Write an *X* in the box if it has six legs. Write an *X* in the box if it has more than six legs.

Bug	Wings	Six Legs	More Than Six Legs
grasshopper			
ant			
ladybug			
caterpillar			
centipede			

ABC Order

Can you put the bug names in ABC order? Look at the first letter of each word. If the letters are the same, look at the next letter. The first one has been done for you.

A B C D E F G H I J K L M N O P Q R S T U V W X Y Z

ant _____   _____   _____   _____

1.RI.1, 1.RI.2, 1.RI.7, 1.RI.9, 1.RI.10, 1.RF.1   CD-104596 • © Carson-Dellosa

Homophones are words that sound the same. They look different. They have different meanings.

Write a sentence with each homophone.

1. be _____

2. bee _____

Qu- sounds like **/kw/**. **Q** is almost always followed by **u**. Circle each **qu-**.

quit   queen   quack

Day 1

Write a sentence with each homophone.

1. one _____

2. won _____

Kn- sounds like **/n/**. Circle each **kn-**.

knit   knife   knight

Day 2

Write a sentence with each homophone.

1. son _____

2. sun _____

Ph- sounds like **/f/**. Circle each **ph-**.

phone   Phil   phrase

Day 3

Write a sentence with each homophone.

1. ate _____

2. eight _____

Wh- sounds like **/hw/**. Circle each **wh-**.

white   what   why

Day 4

Homophones are words that sound the same. They look different. They have different meanings.

1. Draw lines to match the homophones.

aunt	sea
flour	dear
deer	ant
blew	flower
see	blue

2. Write a silly sentence with one pair of homophones.

    Example: The little hare had long pink hair.

    _____

    _____

3. Correct each word. Use the letter pairs in the box.

qu-	kn-	ph-	wh-

A. qwilt _____

B. nock _____

C. foto _____

D. wen _____

Name_____

In the Attic

Ahmad is in a big room. It is on the top floor of his house. It is his attic. It is dark and dusty. Webs are in the corners. Ahmad finds a light. He pulls the string.

1. Where is Ahmad? _____
2. What is the attic like? _____
3. What are in the corners? _____
4. What did Ahmad find? _____

Day 1

Ahmad sees many boxes. He also sees an old rocking chair. He sits in it. It cracks. He jumps! His heart pounds in his chest. He takes a few deep breaths. Then, he feels calm.

1. What did Ahmad see? _____
2. What did Ahmad sit in? _____
3. How do you know he was scared? _____
4. How did he calm down? _____

Day 2

Ahmad sees a big trunk. He puts his hand on the top. It has dust on it. Ahmad wipes the dust off the trunk. He lifts the latch. The trunk opens. Ahmad is surprised.

1. What did Ahmad put his hand on? _____
2. What did Ahmad wipe off? _____
3. What did Ahmad lift? _____
4. Make a prediction. Why is Ahmad surprised? _____

_____

Day 3

Ahmad sees many old picture frames. He picks one up. It is a picture of his dad. His dad is a little boy in the photo. He looks just like Ahmad. Ahmad thought he was looking at himself!

1. What does Ahmad see? _____
2. What did he pick up? _____
3. Who is in the photo? _____
4. What did Ahmad think? _____

Day 4

Exploring

Have you ever gone somewhere and looked around?
Was it a room in your house? Was it a secret place?
What did you find?

1. Write four sentences.

    _____

    _____

    _____

    _____

2. Draw the place.

3. If you found an old trunk like Ahmad did, would you open it? Why or why
    not? Write a sentence. _____

    _____

    _____

1.RL.1, 1.RL.2, 1.RL.3, 1.RL.4, 1.RF.1, 1.RF.4, 1.W.3

Name_____

Write the correct types of words in each column.

NOUN person, place, thing, or idea	VERB action word	ADJECTIVE describing word
apple	run	small

Day 1

Write the correct types of words in each column.

NOUN person, place, thing, or idea	VERB action word	ADJECTIVE describing word
Betty	knock	shiny

Day 2

Write the correct types of words in each column.

NOUN person, place, thing, or idea	VERB action word	ADJECTIVE describing word
Vermont	jumps	blue

Day 3

Write the correct types of words in each column.

NOUN person, place, thing, or idea	VERB action word	ADJECTIVE describing word
hill	walked	deep

Day 4

Silly Paragraph

A paragraph is a group of sentences. Complete the paragraph with words from the previous page. The paragraph may sound silly!

Ramona wants to _____ to her friend's house. Her friend's name is
          (verb)

Bill. Ramona rides her _____ down the street. She _____ and
                 (noun)   (verb)

looks both ways. She is very _____. Then, she gets on the sidewalk and
                      (adjective)

_____ her _____. She sees Bill's _____. His mom is in the
   (verb)   (noun)   (noun)

_____. She waves at Ramona. Ramona _____ and puts her
   (noun)   (verb)

bike in the _____. She is at her friend's house!
              (noun)

1.RF.4, 1.L.1, 1.L.2, 1.L.4

CD-104596 • © Carson-Dellosa

Name_____

Global Warming

We live on Earth. Plants and animals live on Earth. It is important to take care of the planet. Too much trash and gas could harm Earth. It will get warmer. Global warming means that the planet is getting warmer.

1. Where do we live? _____
2. What do we need to take care of? _____
3. What could harm Earth? _____
4. What is global warming? _____

People read about global warming. It is in newspapers and books. People do not want Earth to be too warm. The weather changes. The animals move. Some deer moved north to where it is cooler.

1. Where do people read about global warming? _____
2. What changes? _____
3. What do animals do? _____
4. Where did some deer move? _____

We can fix global warming. We can turn off the water when we brush our teeth. We can turn off the lights when we leave rooms. We can keep windows and doors closed when it is cold outside.

1. What can we fix? _____
2. What can we do when we brush our teeth? _____
3. What should we turn off when we leave rooms? _____
4. What should we close when it is cold? _____

Trash is in landfills. A landfill is a big pile of waste. Paper is in landfills. Plastic is in landfills. Landfills make gas. We can recycle. When we recycle, the waste is used again. We do not have to put all trash in landfills.

1. What is a **landfill**? _____
2. What is in landfills? _____
3. What do landfills make? _____
4. What happens when we recycle? _____

Brainstorm

The theme is the main idea. When you brainstorm, you write. You write about the theme.

1. Add to the theme of **storms**. Write the names of different kinds of storms.

Kinds of Storms

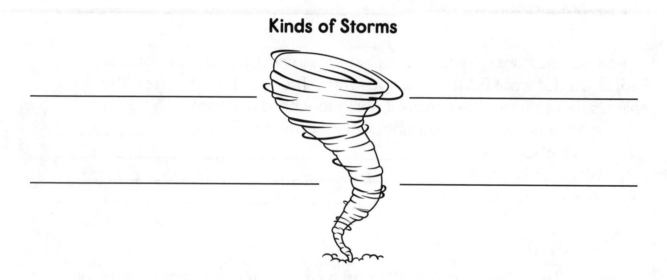

_____   _____

_____   _____

2. Add to the theme of **trash**. Write names of things found in the trash.

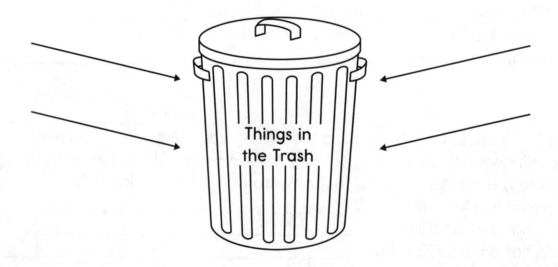

Things in
the Trash

A prefix is a word part. It is at the beginning of a word. **Pre-** means **before**. Write what each word means. The first one has been done for you.

1. pretest   test before
2. preteach   _____
3. precook   _____
4. preheat   _____

Write the lowercase letters.

A ____   B ____   C ____   D ____   E ____   F ____

Day 1

Dis- means **not**. Write what each word means. The first one has been done for you.

1. disagree   not agree
2. dishonest   _____
3. disobey   _____
4. dislike   _____

Write the lowercase letters.

G ____   H ____   I ____   J ____   K ____   L ____

Day 2

Re- means **again**. Write what each word means. The first one has been done for you.

1. retest   test again
2. retell   _____
3. repack   _____
4. repay   _____

Write the lowercase letters.

M ____   N ____   O ____   P ____   Q ____   R ____   S ____

Day 3

Un- means **not**. Write what each word means. The first one has been done for you.

1. unhappy   not happy
2. unlike   _____
3. unable   _____
4. unsure   _____

Write the lowercase letters.

T ____   U ____   V ____   W ____   X ____   Y ____   Z ____

Day 4

Word Parts

A prefix is a part of a word. It is at the beginning.

1. Draw a line to match each prefix to the correct meaning.

    dis-   before
    un-   not
    re-   not
    pre-   again

Word Math

Prefix + Word = Meaning
Write the meaning of each new word.

2. dis + agree = _____

3. un + certain = _____

4. re + name = _____

5. pre + school = _____

ABC Soup

6. Draw lines to match each uppercase letter to its lowercase letter.

Name_____

Where Is My Cat?

Josie and Paws play with yarn. Josie tosses up the yarn. Paws jumps for it! Josie rolls it on the floor. Paws gets ready to pounce! Josie and Paws are good friends. Paws likes it when Josie brushes his fur. It makes Paws purr.

1. Who is Paws? _____
2. What does Josie do with the yarn? _____
3. What does Paws like? _____
4. Do you have an animal friend? Write a sentence. _____
_____

Day 1

Josie gets ready for bed. She is tired. She puts on her pajamas. Paws is under her bed. He hops out and jumps on Josie's pant leg. Josie screams! Paws surprised her. Then, Josie sees Paws run out of her room.

1. What did Josie put on? _____
2. Where was Paws? _____
3. What did Josie do? _____
4. Why do you think Paws ran? Write a sentence. _____
_____

Day 2

In the morning, Josie woke up. She got out of bed. Josie called for Paws. He did not answer. Josie looked in the hallway. He was not there. Josie poured water into his bowl. He did not come to drink it. Josie was worried.

1. What did Josie do in the morning? _____
2. Where did she look for Paws? _____
3. What did she pour into the bowl? _____
4. Why do you think Josie was worried? Write a sentence. _____
_____

Day 3

Paws was under the porch. It began to snow. Paws was cold. He did not want to go inside. He did not want to scare Josie again. Josie opened the porch door. She called for Paws. She heard a *meow*. She looked under the porch. She found him! Josie gave him a hug.

1. Where was Paws? _____
2. Why did Paws not go inside? _____
3. What did Josie open? _____
4. Why did Josie hug Paws? Write a sentence. _____
_____

Day 4

Lost and Found

1. Have you ever lost something? _____

   If yes, answer question 2.   If no, answer question 3.

2. What did you lose? Write a sentence.

   _____

   _____

3. Do you know someone who has lost something? Write a sentence about what he or she lost.

   _____

   _____

   Draw a picture of what the person lost.

4. How do you find something that is lost? Write a sentence.

   _____

   _____

5. What would you do if you found something valuable? Write a sentence.

   _____

   _____

1.RL.1, 1.RL.2, 1.RL.3, 1.RL.4, 1.RF.4, 1.W.3

The names of days and months are proper nouns. They are capitalized.
Rewrite each word, beginning with a capital letter.

1. march _____
2. february _____
3. thursday _____
4. saturday _____

Write a question mark at the end of each asking sentence.

5. When will Ryan get home
6. Where is he

Rewrite each word, beginning with a capital letter.

1. sunday _____
2. may _____
3. september _____
4. december _____

Write a question mark at the end of each asking sentence.

5. Will we bake a cake
6. Do we have eggs

Rewrite each word, beginning with a capital letter.

1. wednesday _____
2. monday _____
3. november _____
4. april _____

Write a question mark at the end of each asking sentence.

5. What time do you go to school
6. What time is lunch

Rewrite each word, beginning with a capital letter.

1. friday _____
2. tuesday _____
3. june _____
4. july _____

Write a question mark at the end of each asking sentence.

5. When does Paul get home
6. Will we see the car

Day 1

Day 2

Day 3

Day 4

Missing Letters

1. Write the missing letters to complete the days and the months.

   S_____nd_____y   Apr_____l

   M_____nd_____y   M_____y

   Tu_____sd_____y   J_____ne

   We_____ne_____day   Jul_____

   T_____ur_____day   Aug_____st

   F_____i_____ay   S_____ptember

   Sa_____ur_____ay   Oct_____ber

   J_____nuary   N_____vember

   F_____bruary   D_____cember

   M_____rch

Ending Punctuation

Write a period at the end of each telling sentence. Write a question mark at the end of each asking sentence.

2. She woke up early today

3. Do you know what time it is

4. It was six o'clock

5. Is she going to eat breakfast

Name_____

Sheepdogs

Sheepdogs are caring. They like to exercise and run. They enjoy being inside and outside. Sheepdogs are good pets for families. They are loving. They protect family members.

1. What are sheepdogs like? _____
2. What do sheepdogs like to do? _____
3. Whom do sheepdogs protect? _____
4. Do you know someone who has a dog? Write a sentence. _____
_____

Sheepdogs need to herd. Herding is when an animal helps move other animals. Sheepdogs are known to herd animals such as sheep and cows. Sheepdogs will even herd family members! They will nudge family members out of danger.

1. What is **herding**? _____
2. What are sheepdogs known to do? _____
3. What will a sheepdog do for a family member? _____
4. Do you know any rescue dogs? Write a sentence. _____
_____

Sheepdogs are from England. They have long fur, so they need to be brushed often. They are strong dogs and love to work. They need a lot of activity. Sheepdogs like to play and run outside.

1. Where are sheepdogs from? _____
2. What needs to be done to their fur? _____
3. What do they love? _____
4. What do they like? Write a sentence. _____
_____

Sheepdogs were used by farmers long ago. The farmers needed dogs to herd animals. Sheepdogs helped them. Sheepdogs are quick and smart. Today, many people have sheepdogs as pets and helpers.

1. Who used sheepdogs long ago? _____
2. What did farmers need? _____
3. Why do you think farmers like sheepdogs? _____
4. An author wrote this story. Does the author think sheepdogs are useful? _____

Helpful Animals

Animals are known to help people. They have helped people for hundreds of years.

Draw lines to match the animals to the correct jobs.

dogs	catch mice
horses	herd sheep
cows	lay eggs
chickens	pull carts
cats	give milk

Write a story about an animal that helped a person. The story can be real or pretend. Write four sentences.

_____

_____

_____

_____

_____

_____

Write a closing sentence. It ends the story.

_____

_____

1.RI.1, 1.RI.2, 1.RI.3, 1.RI.8, 1.RI.10, 1.W.2, 1.W.3

-Ew makes the sound **/oo̅/** as in **few**. Add **-ew** to each blend.

1. fl _____
2. st _____
3. gr_____

An apostrophe shows belonging. Add an apostrophe before **s**.
Example: Amy's cat has stripes. The cat belongs to Amy.

4. Stans dad washed windows.
5. His dads towel was wet.
6. Moms car windows were dirty.

Day 1

-Ue makes the sound **/oo̅/** as in **clue**. Add **-ue** to each blend.

1. bl _____
2. gl _____
3. tr _____

An apostrophe shows belonging. Add an apostrophe before **s**.

4. Marios mom is making dinner.
5. Moms cooking is delicious.
6. Uncle Todds tummy is grumbling.

Day 2

Oo makes the sound **/oo̅/** as in **loop**. Add **oo** to complete each word.

1. st _____p
2. t _____t
3. sw _____p

An apostrophe shows belonging. Add an apostrophe before **s**.

4. Emmas friend lives down the street.
5. Kelseys bike needs to be fixed.
6. Her dads tools are in the house.

Day 3

Oo makes the sound **/o͝o/** as in **look**. Add **oo** to compete each word.

1. br_____k
2. t _____k
3. b_____k

An apostrophe shows belonging. Add an apostrophe before **s**.

4. Drews porch has a grill on it.
5. His aunts deck has a table.
6. His neighbors patio has chairs.

Day 4

All Kinds of Sounds

Complete each word with the correct letters.

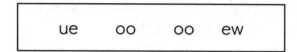

| ue | oo | oo | ew |

1. The bl_____ sky was beautiful.

2. The tree has r_____ts.

3. The breeze bl_____ the trees.

4. It is fun to l_____k at the clouds.

Ownership

Apostrophes show ownership. When a word has an apostrophe, it "owns something." Add the apostrophes.

5. Chandras favorite food is ice cream.

6. Jennas best friend is coming over.

7. Kyles brother is at a party.

8. Jeffreys class is near the library.

9. What is your friend's favorite day? Why? Write two sentences.

_____

_____

  CD-104596 • © Carson-Dellosa

Name_____

Sisters

   Natalie and Bridget are sisters. They enjoy contests. They like to have contests in their backyard. Natalie and Bridget have new kites from the store. They want to fly the kites.

1. Who are Natalie and Bridget? _____
2. What do they enjoy? _____
3. Where do they have contests? _____
4. What did they get from the store? _____

   The girls wait for a windy day. When the wind is strong, they bring their kites outside. Natalie wants her kite to fly the highest. Bridget says her kite will fly higher! The girls let the kites go into the air.

1. What did the girls wait for? _____
2. When did they bring their kites outside? _____
3. What did Natalie want? _____
4. Where do the kites go? _____

   The kites are high in the air. The girls hold the end of the strings. Bridget's kite is higher than Natalie's. Suddenly, Natalie's kite spins around. It crashes to the ground. Bridget asks Natalie if she wants to try again.

1. What did the girls hold? _____
2. Whose kite was higher? _____
3. What happened to Natalie's kite? _____
4. What did Bridget ask Natalie? _____

   Bridget looks at her kite. A breeze spins her kite around! It flies into a tree. The kite is stuck! Natalie runs over to help Bridget get her kite out of the tree. They tug at the string, and the kite falls out of the tree. The two girls look at each other and laugh. What a windy day!

1. What happened to Bridget's kite? _____
2. What did Natalie do? _____
3. What did the girls do to get the kite down? _____
4. What kind of day was it? _____

Name_____

Adjectives are describing words.

Loud is an adjective.

If you add **-er** to the end of **loud**, you make it **louder**.
If you add **-est** to the end of **loud**, you make it the **loudest**!

Make each adjective stronger with **-er**.
Then, make it strongest with **-est**.

light   tight

light_____   tight_____

light_____   tight_____

small   great

small_____   great_____

small_____   great_____

long   slow

long_____   slow_____

long_____   slow_____

Write three sentences. The first sentence should have the word **warm**. The second sentence should have the word **warmer**. The third sentence should have the word **warmest**.

1. _____

2. _____

3. _____

1.RL.1, 1.RL.2, 1.RL.3, 1.RL.9, 1.RF.4, 1.L.5   CD-104596 • © Carson-Dellosa

To, **two**, and **too** each mean something different. Use the correct word in each sentence.
1. We went _____ the house.
2. There are _____ kids in the yard.
3. We will play at the house _____.

A pronoun takes the place of a noun. Write the correct pronoun in each sentence.
4. Leila sits in a chair. _____ has a big pillow.
5. Mario goes to the store. _____ rides his bike there.

To, **two**, and **too** each mean something different. Use the correct word in each sentence.
1. I went _____ my new school.
2. I have _____ teachers in my classroom.
3. They teach music _____.

Write the correct pronoun in each sentence.
4. Dr. Chen goes to her work. _____ rides the train.
5. Will eats bananas. _____ loves them.

There, **their**, and **they're** each mean something different. Use the correct word in each sentence.
1. Jessi went to _____ party.
2. Many other children were _____.
3. She hopes _____ happy with her gifts.

Write the correct pronoun in each sentence.
4. Lynn and Maurice get to go on a trip. _____ are happy.
5. Gabe will meet the principal. _____ is going to wait in the office.

There, **their**, and **they're** each mean something different. Use the correct word in each sentence.
1. _____ going to see a movie.
2. The theater is in _____ town.
3. It is on the street over _____.

Write the correct pronoun in each sentence.
4. Kayla and I are walking. _____ are going to the park.
5. Marcus and Ben went to the library. _____ rode their scooters there.

To, Two, Too

To, **two**, and **too** sound the same. But, they are different. Use each word in a sentence.

1. _____

2. _____

3. _____

There, **their**, and **they're** sound the same. But, they are different. Use each word in a sentence.

4. _____

5. _____

6. _____

A pronoun takes the place of a noun. Write each sentence again using a pronoun instead of a noun.

7. Corinna saw a swan. _____

8. Danielle caught a fish. _____

9. Miguel and Juan went swimming. _____

Name_____

Bumps!

Emma woke up. She was still tired. She had not slept very well. She got out of bed and put on her slippers. She walked to the bathroom. She got her toothbrush and put toothpaste on it. She began to brush her teeth. She looked in the mirror. She was surprised!

1. How did Emma feel when she woke up? _____
2. What did she do first when she got out of bed? _____
3. What did she do in the bathroom? _____
4. Why do you think Emma was surprised? _____

When she looked in the mirror, she saw pink bumps on her cheeks. Her face was red. The bumps felt itchy. She tried not to scratch them. She asked her mom to come quickly.

1. What did Emma see? _____
2. What color was her face? _____
3. How did the bumps feel? _____
4. What do you think she will tell her mom? _____

_____

Emma's mom went upstairs. She walked into the bathroom. She saw Emma's face. Emma was worried. Her mom told her not to worry. Her mom called the doctor. Emma went back into her room and got dressed. Emma's mom drove her to the doctor.

1. How did Emma feel? _____
2. What did her mom do? _____
3. Where did Emma and her mom go? _____
4. What do you think the doctor will say? _____

Emma and her mom waited in the doctor's office. The nurse called for Emma and her mom. The doctor came in. The doctor said that Emma needed a special cream. She and her mom went to get the cream. Emma's mom put it on Emma's face right away. Emma felt better.

1. Where did Emma and her mom wait? _____
2. What did the doctor say Emma needed? _____
3. When did Emma's mom put the cream on Emma? _____
4. Did you ever go to the doctor? Write a sentence. _____

_____

73

A story has a beginning, a middle, and an end. The beginning catches your attention. It makes you want to read the story. It tells about the main idea of the story. The middle is full of details. It tells about the main idea. The end closes the story. It makes you think.

Write the beginning of a story. Write two sentences. Catch the reader's attention.

_____

_____

_____

Write the middle of the story. Write five sentences. Give details about your main idea.

_____

_____

_____

_____

Write the end of the story. It can be one or two sentences. Close the story.

_____

_____

Read your story to a classmate or an adult.

1.RL.1, 1.RL.2, 1.RL.3, 1.RL.4, 1.RF.4, 1.W.3, 1.W.5

Sight words are words you see often. Put the sight words in ABC order.

ask   have   just   give   after

_____   _____   _____   _____   _____

The letter **c** has two sounds. There is a soft **c** (**/s/**) as in **ice** and a hard **c** (**/k/**) as in **case**.

Which **c** do you hear—soft or hard?

1. cent _____
2. coat _____

Day 1

Sight words are words you see often. Put the sight words in ABC order.

jump   when   out   all   take

_____   _____   _____   _____   _____

The letter **c** has two sounds. There is a soft **c** (**/s/**) as in **ice** and a hard **c** (**/k/**) as in **case**.

Which **c** do you hear—soft or hard?

1. cat _____
2. cement _____

Day 2

Sight words are words you see often. Put the sight words in ABC order.

open   some   stop   let   old

_____   _____   _____   _____   _____

The letter **g** has two sounds. There is a soft **g** (**/j/**) as in **gem** and a hard **g** (**/g/**) as in **girl**.

Which **g** do you hear—soft or hard?

1. goat _____
2. giant _____

Day 3

Sight words are words you see often. Put the sight words in ABC order.

get   up   walk   come   first

_____   _____   _____   _____   _____

The letter **g** has two sounds. There is a soft **g** (**/j/**) as in **gem** and a hard **g** (**/g/**) as in **girl**.

Which **g** do you hear—soft or hard?

1. gift _____
2. gentle _____

Day 4

Sight Words

Sight words are useful words. You see them every day. Write the sight words in ABC order on each train.

about   think   five   then   his

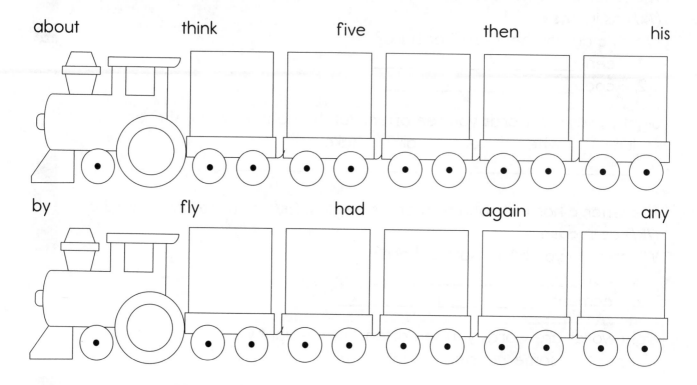

by   fly   had   again   any

Hard and Soft Sounds

Write the **hard c** and **g** words on the rock. Write the **soft c** and **g** words on the pillow.

cap
catch
cell
center
cup
germ
get
giraffe
Gus
gust

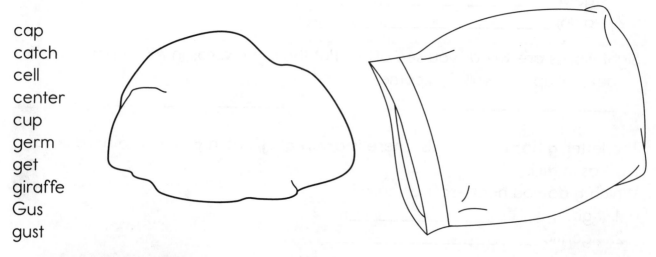

1.RF.2, 1.RF.3, 1.L.2, 1.L.6

Name_____

Tornadoes

   A tornado is a large storm. It starts on land. It has strong winds. Thunderstorms happen. The air begins to spin. The air becomes a funnel. A funnel is a tube.

1.   What is a **tornado**? _____
2.   Where does it start? _____
3.   What does the air do? _____
4.   What is a **funnel**? _____

   A tornado's funnel is powerful. It moves things with wind power. It can even move a house or a car! Tornadoes do not happen very often. When they happen, we must be careful.

1.   What is powerful? _____
2.   What can tornadoes move? _____
3.   When do tornadoes happen? _____
4.   Have you ever seen a tornado? Write a sentence. _____
   _____

   It is important to be safe when a tornado is near. The best place to be is in a basement. If no basement is available, it is best to go to the middle of a house or a building and to stay away from windows. If outside, it is best to go to a ditch or lie low on the ground.

1.   Where is the best place to be? _____
2.   Where should we go if no basement is available? _____
3.   What should we stay away from? _____
4.   Where should we go if we are outside? _____

   Tornadoes are also called twisters. They can have winds that reach 100 miles per hour. That is faster than some cars go. Weather radar finds tornadoes. The radar follows tornadoes' paths.

1.   What else are tornadoes called? _____
2.   How fast can the winds be? _____
3.   What does weather radar find? _____
4.   What does weather radar follow? _____

Extra! Extra!

A newspaper tells many stories. Some stories have facts. They are true. Other stories are opinions. They tell how people feel. These stories do not always have facts. Create your own newspaper. Then, type your newspaper on a computer.

Name your newspaper.	
Write a factual story. It is a true story. _____ _____ _____ _____ _____	Draw a picture for the story.
Write an opinion story. It is not a true story. It is how you feel about something. _____ _____ _____ _____	Draw a picture for the story.

1.RL.1, 1.RL.2, 1.RL.4, 1.RL.5, 1.RF.4, 1.W.1, 1.W.3, 1.W.6

A suffix is a word part. It is at the end of a word. **-Ful** means **full of**. Write what each word means. The first one has been done for you.

1. graceful   full of grace
2. cheerful   _____
3. painful   _____
4. useful   _____

Circle the three color words.

purple   free   red   when   house   blue   paper

Day 1

-Ful means **full of**. Write what each word means. The first one has been done for you.

1. careful   full of care
2. joyful   _____
3. fearful   _____
4. colorful   _____

Circle the three food words.

popcorn   truck   carrot   bread   frame   hair   yellow

Day 2

-Er means **one who**. Write what each word means. The first one has been done for you.

1. painter   one who paints
2. seller   _____
3. bowler   _____
4. driver   _____

Circle the three animal words.

smile   pine   deer   lion   towel   cheek   dog

Day 3

-Er means **one who**. Write what each word means. The first one has been done for you.

1. teacher   one who teaches
2. server   _____
3. diver   _____
4. baker   _____

Circle the three body words.

swings   horse   slide   nose   leg   six   arm

Day 4

Add the suffix **-er** or **-ful** to the end of each word.

1. thank_____

2. harm_____

3. call_____

4. farm_____

5. dream_____

6. peace_____

7. truth_____

8. sing_____

Write each word in the correct shopping bag.

shirt   salad   beans   pants   rice   socks   shorts   meat   hat   yogurt

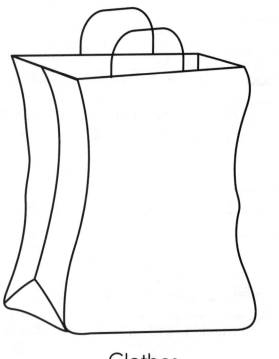

Clothes

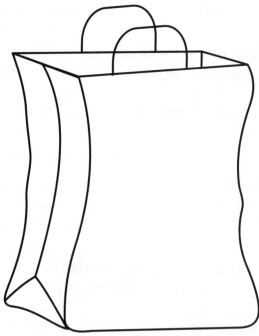

Food

Name_____

Animal Shelter

Jose volunteers at an animal shelter. The shelter is full of dogs and cats. They are waiting to find loving homes. Jose takes care of the cats and the dogs. He feeds them. He gives them baths.

Retell the story in your own words. Write two or more sentences.

_____
_____
_____

Day 1

Bird-watching

Victoria is a bird-watcher. She looks at birds from her window. She has many bird feeders. Victoria gives the birds seed to eat. They also like cracked corn. Victoria takes pictures of the birds.

Retell the story in your own words. Write two or more sentences.

_____
_____
_____

Day 2

Dog Walking

Daysha is a dog walker. She gets home from school and does her homework. Then, she goes to her neighbor's house. Neo waits for her at the door. She puts a leash on him. The dog is very friendly.

Retell the story in your own words. Write two or more sentences.

_____
_____
_____

Day 3

Truck Fun

Darron loves trucks. He goes to his dad's job on the weekends. Darron watches the trucks. Sometimes, he can sit on the bulldozer. He likes to watch the trucks move dirt.

Retell the story in your own words. Write two or more sentences.

_____
_____
_____

Day 4

When you retell a story, you put it in your own words. Retell the stories below. Write two or more sentences for each story. Then, type your sentences on a computer.

1. Ethan visits his grandmother. She is in a special home. Nurses take care of her. She likes when Ethan comes to visit. They play checkers together.

_____

_____

_____

_____

2. Alicia moved from Texas. Now, she lives in New York. Alicia is happy in New York. Her new school and friends are nice. Alicia writes to her friends in Texas. They talk on the phone too.

_____

_____

_____

_____

3. Carla lives on a farm. She takes care of the horses. She wakes up early to open the barn. She feeds the horses and puts them in the stable. The stable is where the horses live. She fills their buckets with water. Then, she goes to school.

_____

_____

_____

_____

A digraph is two letters that make a new sound. **Sh** is a digraph. Add **sh** to complete each word. Write the word.

1. _____ip   _____
2. di_____   _____
3. _____in   _____

Synonyms are words that have the same meaning. Match the synonyms.

plate   boat
damp   dish
ship   wet

Day 1

A digraph is two letters that make a new sound. **Ch** is a digraph. Add **ch** to complete each word. Write the word.

1. _____ip   _____
2. _____op   _____
3. _____in   _____

Synonyms are words that have the same meaning. Match the synonyms.

paste   hope
wish   glue
like   enjoy

Day 2

A digraph is two letters that make a new sound. **Th** is a digraph. Add **th** to complete each word. Write the word.

1. _____is   _____
2. wi_____   _____
3. _____in   _____

Synonyms are words that have the same meaning. Match the synonyms.

pal   cab
cool   friend
taxi   chilly

Day 3

A digraph is two letters that make a new sound. **Wh** is a digraph. Add **wh** to complete each word. Write the word.

1. _____ite   _____
2. _____en   _____
3. _____irl   _____

Synonyms are words that have the same meaning. Match the synonyms.

unhappy   giggle
laugh   sad
smile   grin

Day 4

Name_____

Write the missing digraphs.

| ch | sh | th | wh |

1. Yasmin walks on the sandy bea_____.

2. She collects sea_____ells.

3. She likes _____at purple shell the most.

4. _____en her hands are full, she puts the shells in a bucket.

Synonyms are words that have the same meaning. Write a synonym for each word.

5. kids _____

6. ladies _____

7. noisy _____

8. center _____

9. kind _____

10. begin _____

11. Fill in the first set of blanks with a friend. Then, write words that have the same meaning. Example: Wind is the same as breeze.

_____ is the same as _____.

_____ is the same as _____.

_____ is the same as _____.

_____ is the same as _____.

Spencer's Chores

Spencer's room was a mess. His clothes were on the floor. His shoes were on the desk. Spencer even had a plate of old food on his bed. His mom told him that it is time to do chores.

1. What were on the floor? _____
2. Where were Spencer's shoes? _____
3. What was on his bed? _____
4. What did his mom tell him?_____

Day 1

Spencer was angry. He did not want to do chores. He thought chores were not fun. He wanted to play outside instead. His friends were waiting for him in the yard.

1. Why was Spencer angry? _____
2. What did he think of chores? _____
3. What did he want to do? _____
4. Who was waiting in the yard? _____

Day 2

Spencer's mom went to the door. She told his friends that he was going to clean his room. Spencer could not go outside. His friend Michael said he does chores every week. He gets the mail and sets the table. Jeff said he does chores every day. He takes out the trash and walks the dog.

1. What did Spencer's mom do? _____
2. What did Spencer have to do? _____
3. How often does Michael do chores? _____
4. What chores does Jeff do? _____

Day 3

Spencer heard his friends talk to his mom. Spencer did not know that his friends do chores. Spencer was ready to try his chores. He wrote a to-do list. It said he would make his bed and pick up his clothes. He would throw out the old food and move the shoes. Then, his room would be clean!

1. What did Spencer hear?_____
2. What did Spencer learn about his friends? _____
3. What did Spencer write? _____
4. What was on the list? _____

Day 4

Are Chores Good or Bad?

Some kids think chores are not fun. They do not want to do chores at all. Other kids like chores. They like to help keep rooms clean.

1. What is your opinion of chores? Do you like them or not?

    _____

    _____

2. Why do you feel this way?

    _____

    _____

3. Do you do chores at home? _____

Write four sentences about your feelings on junk food. Start with your opinion. How do you feel? Give two reasons for your opinion. End your writing with one sentence.

_____

_____

_____

_____

1.RL.1, 1.RL.2, 1.RL.9, 1.W.1, 1.W.8

When you edit a sentence, you correct it.
Rewrite each sentence. Correct the three mistakes in each one.

1. mariah wants two get a new pet

2. her Aunt lisa does not want a cat or a dog

3. maybe they con get a fish

4. fish are easy to take cure of

Day 1

When you edit a sentence, you correct it.
Rewrite each sentence. Correct the three mistakes in each one.

1. shane likes it wen it rains

2. he puts on his big rain bots

3. then, he jums in the puddles

4. he forgets his umbrella all the tim

Day 2

When you edit a sentence, you correct it.
Rewrite each sentence. Correct the three mistakes in each one.

1. casey loves to color wit pencils

2. se makes her drawings colorful

3. she will color for mor than an hour

4. her mom liks to display the drawings

Day 3

When you edit a sentence, you correct it.
Rewrite eack sentence. Correct the three mistakes in each one.

1. jorge did not feel well at scool

2. he went too the nurse's office to rest

3. the nurse called his dad at his jab

4. his dad will com pick him up

Day 4

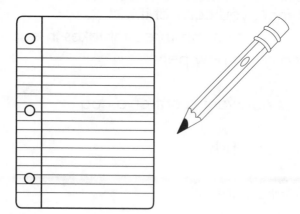

Many people edit sentences. It is a job. Students edit their schoolwork. Newspaper editors edit articles. Teachers edit too.

Jayla wrote a letter to give to her teacher. But, she wants to edit it first. Help her edit the letter and correct the 10 mistakes.

Dear Mrs. Huber,

you are my favorite teacher! I am glad I had you tis year   I will miss you this summer. i will come back two visit you when school starts.

I learned a lot in you class. you are kind and nic. I hop you have a fun summer!

Love,

jayla

1.L.1, 1.L.2

Answer Key

Page 9
Day 1: 1. Answers will vary; 2. Answers will vary; 3. five; 4. In different places, small town, large city; **Day 2:** 1. 15; 2. in a tank; 3. Oscar; 4. He eats lettuce and sits on a rock; **Day 3:** 1. on a busy street in the city; 2. around the outside of the school; 3. Answers will vary; 4. basketball hoop, basketball court, playground, slide, small garden; **Day 4:** 1. Ms. Moore; 2. read, write, do math; 3. be kind and listen; 4. when the class is too noisy

Page 10
1. Myra's art class; 2. narrator; 3. go to art class; 4. A; 5. B; 6. Answers will vary.

Page 11
Day 1: 1. My; 2. cat; 3. period; 4. cat, bath; **Day 2:** 1. We; 2. fish; 3. period; 4. fish, swim; **Day 3:** 1. Jake; 2. mop; 3. period; 4. pond, mop; **Day 4:** 1. The; 2. cup; 3. period; 4. up, run

Page 12
1. Kit; 2. Please; 3. They; 4. duck, sock, apple; 5. rug, box; 6. question mark; 7. period; 8. period; 9. nap; 10. rug

Page 13
Day 1: 1. play with shadows; 2. make shapes on the wall; 3. Answers will vary; **Day 2:** 1. lamps and flashlights; 2. the sun; 3. Answers will vary (a shadow is made by light); **Day 3:** 1. behind you; 2. in front of you; 3. Answers will vary; **Day 4:** 1. pictures and animals; 2. ducks, alligators, rabbits; 3. Answers will vary.

Page 14
1. A; 2. C; 3. B; 4. Answers will vary.

Page 15
Days 1, 2, 3, 4: Nouns will vary; Add **-s** to each word.

Page 16
1. hat, pup, bib, can, bag; 2. Answers will vary; 3. Answers will vary; 4. hats, pups, bibs, cans, bags; 5. Answers will vary.

Page 17
Day 1: 1. Many people in the world; 2. in ponds; 3. rain; 4. Answers will vary; **Day 2:** 1. in thick mud; 2. grass; 3. it bends down; 4. Check students' drawings; **Day 3:** 1. large with patches; 2. holes in the field; 3. a tool; 4. Answers will vary; **Day 4:** 1. hats, bags, rope; 2. help plants grow; 3. medicine; 4. Answers will vary.

Page 18
1. True; 2. True; 3. False; 4. True; 5. False; 6. False; 7. False; 8. True; 9. False; 10. False

Page 19
Days 1, 2, 3, 4: Capitalize the first letter of each proper noun; Add **-e** to the end of each short vowel word to make long vowel words.

Page 20
1. Check students' circling; 2. Matt, Rider, Darius; 3. They start with capital letters, or They are names; 4. mitt, sun, net, crab, box; 5. cake, cane, grapes, lake, gate

Page 21
Day 1: 1. in the ocean; 2. for thousands of years; 3. more than 350 kinds; 4. big or small; **Day 2:** 1. they open their mouths; 2. they can breathe; 3. their teeth; 4. Answers will vary; **Day 3:** 1. long or short, up to 36 feet; 2. a stapler; 3. small sharks; 4. large sharks; **Day 4:** 1. belts; 2. shark meat, shark fin soup; 3. in a net; 4. Answers will vary.

Page 22
1. Mugu Moja; 2. a chimp; 3. Africa; 4. 2007; 5. to save chimps; 6. happy

Page 23
Day 1: 1. rides; 2. holds; 3. smells; 4. sees; 5.–6. bl; **Day 2:** 1. calls; 2. looks; 3. sits; 4. plays; 5.–6. fr; **Day 3:** 1. runs; 2. jumps; 3. finds; 4. lifts; 5.–6. tr; **Day 4:** 1. makes; 2. sells; 3. cleans; 4. swims; 5.–6. st

Page 24
1. Answers will vary (six verbs); 2. Answers will vary; 3. Answers will vary.

Page 25
Day 1: 1. ride a horse; 2. horse books; 3. in art class; 4. Answers will vary; **Day 2:** 1. Liv's aunt; 2. two; 3. Henry; 4. He had brown fur; His eyes were round and black; **Day 3:** 1. soft; 2. if she could feed Henry; 3. stable; 4. He ate fast; **Day 4:** 1. Liv could sit on Henry; 2. jumped up and down; 3. helmet; 4. Answers will vary (students should infer from Liv's smile).

Page 26
1. Answers will vary; 2. Answers will vary; 3. Answers will vary.

Page 27
Day 1: 1. fire; 2. Answers will vary; 3. Answers will vary but may include play, pay, May, say, lay, Fay, ray, bay; Check students' circling; **Day 2:** 1. snowman; 2. Answers will vary; 3. Answers will vary but may include rail, tail, snail, fail, bail, hail, mail, sail; Check students' circling; **Day 3:** 1. teddy bear; 2. Answers will vary; 3. Answers will vary but may include wheat, eat, neat, read; Check students' circling; **Day 4:** 1. rabbit; 2. Answers will vary; 3. Answers will vary but may include bee, fee, tree; Check students' circling.

Page 28
1. blue; 2. furry; 3. tall; 4. stinky; 5. hot; 6.–10. Answers will vary.

Page 29
Day 1: 1. It is a large bird; 2. It can grow to nine feet; 3. It is taller than a man; 4. It is too big; **Day 2:** 1. It can run; 2. 16 feet; 3. It has strong legs; 4. with short wings; **Day 3:** 1. Most birds have four toes; 2. two; 3. four inches; 4. The two toes and the claw dig into the dirt as it runs to get speed; **Day 4:** 1. in the sand; 2. male and female ostriches; 3. up to 60; 4. It takes 40 days for the eggs to hatch.

Answer Key

Page 30
1. tiger, lion, cheetah; 2. Answers will vary but may include tails, fur, look like cats; 3. wolf, coyote, fox; 4. Answers will vary but may include ears, face, howl/bark, look like dogs.

Page 31
Day 1: 1. o; 2. don't; 3. **/ow/** words include now, cow, pow, wow; 4. circle owl, cow; **Day 2:** 1. a; 2. we're; 3. **/ō/** words include mow, bow, low, tow; 4. circle bow, bowl; **Day 3:** 1. o; 2. hadn't; 3. **/ī/** words include fry, my, by, cry; 4. circle fly; **Day 4:** 1. i; 2. she's; 3. **/ē/** words include merry, Kerry, Perry; 4. circle baby

Page 32
1.–5. Answers will vary; **/ow/** towel, tower; **/ō/** flow, blow; **/ī/** my, why; **/ē/** carry, foggy

Page 33
Day 1: 1. her grandmother; 2. actors onstage; 3. bad; 4. dizzy; **Day 2:** 1. actors; 2. said lines, moved onstage, danced, sang; 3. have fun like the actors; 4. someone to help her; **Day 3:** 1. if she could get a teacher; 2. how to act and have fun onstage; 3. called the acting teacher; 4. happy; **Day 4:** 1. a teacher, actor; 2. an actor; 3. help children learn to act onstage; 4. calm and brave

Page 34
1.–4. Answers will vary.

Page 35
Day 1: 1. tiny, miniature; 2. phone or bell sound; **Day 2:** 1. freezing, icy; 2. tells time; **Day 3:** 1. giant, huge; 2. holds soup, container; **Day 4:** 1. shout, yell; 2. small animal

Page 36
1. big/giant, small/tiny, hot/boiling, cold/icy; 2. dog sound; 3. small animal; 4. cardboard, container; 5. cut, trim; 6. group of people

Page 37
Day 1: 1. sweet, sticky; 2. comes from trees; 3. tree needs hole in it; 4. Answers will vary; **Day 2:** 1. hole in the tree; 2. hang buckets on the trees; 3. metal; 4. at the end of the day; **Day 3:** 1. inside; 2. boil the sap; 3. over a fire; 4. turns a dark color; **Day 4:** 1. when the sap turns to syrup; 2. put syrup into bottles; 3. in stores; 4. Answers will vary.

Page 38
1.–5. Answers will vary.

Page 39
Day 1: Answers will vary; 1. kick, will kick; 2. bake, will bake; **Day 2:** Answers will vary; 1. want, will want; 2. laugh, will laugh; **Day 3:** Answers will vary; 1. ask, will ask; 2. work, will work; **Day 4:** Answers will vary; 1. lift, will lift; 2. joke, will joke

Page 40
1. and; 2. but; 3. so; 4. or; 5. future; 6. present; 7. present; 8. future; 9. past; 10. past

Page 41
Day 1: 1. Japan; 2. nature; 3. 17; 4. three;
Day 2: 1. a kigo; 2. a season; 3. spring, summer, autumn, winter; 4. wintertime;
Day 3: 1. nature or animals; 2. does not rhyme; 3. syllable pattern; 4. three;
Day 4: 1. frog; 2. spring or summer; 3. hot, fresh grass, wet mud; 4. 5-7-5

Page 42
Answers will vary. Students should follow a nature or animal theme and the 5-7-5/17 syllable pattern.

Page 43
Day 1: 1.–3. exclamation points should be added; 4. backpack; 5. sunshine;
Day 2: 1.–3. exclamation points should be added; 4. rainbow; 5. eyeball;
Day 3: 1.–3. exclamation points should be added; 4. raincoat; 5. doghouse;
Day 4: 1.–3. exclamation points should be added; 4. sleepwalk; 5. lifeguard

Page 44
1.–3. Answers will vary; 4.–10. grasshopper, schoolhouse, skateboard, afternoon, without

Page 45
Day 1: 1. She needed help; 2. It helps her walk; 3. They help her see; 4. It helps her hear; **Day 2:** 1. her hearing aid; 2. I have to speak up; 3. talking louder; 4. Answers will vary; **Day 3:** 1. the kitchen; 2. family; 3. a cherry pie; 4. Answers will vary; **Day 4:** 1. bake; 2. spoon; 3. blueberry; 4. flour, water, eggs, sugar

Page 46
1.–3. Answers will vary.

Page 47
Day 1: bump rhymes with lump, jump; camp rhymes with lamp, ramp; circle the **oa**;
Day 2: land rhymes with hand, band; sound rhymes with pound, round; circle the **oe**;
Day 3: bank rhymes with sank, tank; sink rhymes with mink, link; circle the **ie**;
Day 4: fast rhymes with last, cast; rust rhymes with must, gust; circle the **uy**

Page 48
1. Circle pl-, sh-, fl-; 2. Answers will vary;
3. Circle -nt, -nt, -mp; 4. Answers will vary;
5. boat, soap, goat, toe

Page 49
Day 1: 1. many places; 2. 5,000; 3. red with black spots; 4. Ladybugs eat pests on farm crops; **Day 2:** 1. six; 2. a shell; 3. birds; 4. It can play dead; **Day 3:** 1. on a leaf; 2. larvae; 3. skin; 4. on a leaf; **Day 4:** 1. Europe; 2. more than 100 years ago; 3. many different places, like forests; 4. hide in warm places, rest under rocks and logs

Page 50
grasshopper—wings, six legs; Ant—six legs; Ladybug—wings, six legs; Caterpillar—more than six legs; Centipede—more than six legs; ABC order—ant, caterpillar, centipede, grasshopper, ladybug

Page 51
Day 1: 1.–2. Answers will vary; Circle the **qu**;
Day 2: 1.–2. Answers will vary; Circle the **kn**;
Day 3: 1.–2. Answers will vary; Circle the **ph**;
Day 4: 1.–2. Answers will vary; Circle the **wh**

Page 52
1. aunt/ant, flour/flower, deer/dear, blew/blue, see/sea; 2. Answers will vary; 3. quilt, knock, photo, when

Page 53
Day 1: 1. in a big room, his attic; 2. dark, dusty; 3. webs; 4. a light; **Day 2:** 1. many boxes; 2. old rocking chair; 3. he jumped; 4. he took a few deep breaths; **Day 3:** 1. a big trunk; 2. dust; 3. latch; 4. Answers will vary; **Day 4:** 1. many old picture frames; 2. picture; 3. his dad as a little boy; 4. that his dad looks like him

Page 54
1.–3. Answers will vary.

Page 55
Days 1, 2, 3, 4: Answers will vary.

Page 56
Answers will vary.

Page 57
Day 1: 1. Earth; 2. planet Earth; 3. too much trash and gas; 4. Earth is getting warmer; **Day 2:** 1. in newspapers and books; 2. the weather; 3. move; 4. north to where it was cooler; **Day 3:** 1. global warming; 2. turn off water; 3. lights; 4. windows and doors; **Day 4:** 1. big pile of waste; 2. paper, plastic; 3. gas; 4. The waste is used again.

Page 58
1.–2. Answers will vary.

Page 59
Day 1: 2. teach before; 3. cook before; 4. heat before; a, b, c, d, e, f; **Day 2:** 2. not honest; 3. not obey; 4. not like; g, h, i, j, k, l; **Day 3:** 2. tell again; 3. pack again; 4. pay again; m, n, o, p, q, r, s; **Day 4:** 2. not like; 3. not able; 4. not sure; t, u, v, w, x, y, z

Page 60
1. dis/not, un/not, re/again, pre/before; 2. not agree; 3. not certain; 4. name again; 5. before school; 6. Bb, Dd, Ff, Gg, Pp, Zz

Page 61
Day 1: 1. Paws is a cat; 2. tosses it up; 3. when Josie brushes her fur; 4. Answers will vary; **Day 2:** 1. pajamas; 2. under the bed; 3. screamed; 4. Answers will vary; **Day 3:** 1. woke up, got out of bed; 2. hallway; 3. water; 4. Answers will vary; **Day 4:** 1. under the porch; 2. He did not want to scare Josie again; 3. the porch door; 4. Answers will vary.

Page 62
1.–5. Answers will vary.

Page 63
Day 1: 1.–4. Capitalize the first letters; 5.–6. Add question marks at the ends; **Day 2:** 1.–4. Capitalize first letters; 5.–6. Add question marks at the ends; **Day 3:** 1.–4. Capitalize first letters; 5.–6. Add question marks at the ends; **Day 4:** 1.–4. Capitalize first letters; 5.–6. Add question marks at the ends

Page 64
1. Sunday, Monday, Tuesday, Wednesday, Thursday, Friday, Saturday; January, February, March, April, May, June, July, August, September, October, November, December; 2. period; 3. question mark; 4. period; 5. question mark

Page 65
Day 1: 1. caring; 2. exercise and run; 3. family members; 4. Answers will vary; **Day 2:** 1. when an animal helps move other animals; 2. herd animals such as sheep and cows; 3. nudge a family member out of danger; 4. Answers will vary; **Day 3:** 1. England; 2. brushed; 3. work; 4. They like to play and run outside; **Day 4:** 1. farmers; 2. a dog to herd animals; 3. They are quick and smart; 4. Answers will vary.

Page 66
dogs/herd sheep, horses/pull carts, cows/give milk, chickens/lay eggs, cats/catch mice; Answers will vary.

Page 67
Day 1: 1. flew; 2. stew; 3. grew; 4. Stan's; 5. dad's; 6. Mom's; **Day 2:** 1. blue; 2. glue; 3. true; 4. Mario's; 5. Mom's; 6. Todd's; **Day 3:** 1. stoop; 2. toot; 3. swoop; 4. Emma's; 5. Kelsey's; 6. dad's; **Day 4:** 1. brook; 2. took; 3. book; 4. Drew's; 5. aunt's; 6. neighbor's

Page 68
1. ue; 2. oo; 3. ew; 4. oo; 5. Chandra's; 6. Jenna's; 7. Kyle's; 8. Jeffrey's; 9. Stories will vary—encourage each student to ask a classmate about a favorite day.

Page 69
Day 1: 1. They are sisters; 2. contests; 3. their backyard; 4. new kites; **Day 2:** 1. a windy day; 2. when the wind was strong; 3. her kite to fly the highest; 4. into the air; **Day 3:** 1. strings; 2. Bridget's; 3. it crashed to the ground; 4. if she wanted to try again; **Day 4:** 1. flew into a tree; 2. help Bridget; 3. tug at the string; 4. windy

Page 70
Lighter, lightest; smaller, smallest; longer, longest; tighter, tightest; greater, greatest; slower, slowest; 1.–3. Check students' answers.

Page 71
Day 1: 1. to; 2. two; 3. too; 4. It; 5. He; **Day 2:** 1. to; 2. two; 3. too; 4. She; 5. He; **Day 3:** 1. their; 2. there; 3. they're; 4. They; 5. He; **Day 4:** 1. They're; 2. their; 3. there; 4. We; 5. They

Page 72
1.–6. Answers will vary; 7. She saw a swan; 8. She caught a fish; 9. They went swimming.

Page 73
Day 1: 1. tired; 2. put on her slippers; 3. got her toothbrush and put toothpaste on it; 4. Answers will vary; **Day 2:** 1. pink bumps; 2. red; 3. itchy; 4. Answers will vary; **Day 3:** 1. worried; 2. told her not to worry, called the doctor; 3. to the doctor; 4. Answers will vary; **Day 4:** 1. in the doctor's office; 2. special cream; 3. right away; 4. Answers will vary.

Page 74
Answers will vary.

Page 75
Day 1: after, ask, give, have, just; 1. soft c; 2. hard c; **Day 2:** all, jump, out, take, when; 1. hard c; 2. soft c; **Day 3:** let, old, open, some, stop; 1. hard g; 2. soft g; **Day 4:** come, first, get, up, walk; 1. hard g; 2. soft g

Page 76
about, five, his, then, think; again, any, by, fly, had; Rock—cap, get, Gus, cup, gust, catch; Pillow—cell, germ, center, giraffe

Page 77
Day 1: 1. large storm; 2. on land; 3. spins, becomes a funnel; 4. tube; **Day 2:** 1. tornado's funnel; 2. house, car; 3. not very often; 4. Answers will vary; **Day 3:** 1. a basement; 2. middle of a house or a building; 3. windows; 4. ditch or lie low on ground; **Day 4:** 1. twisters; 2. 100 miles per hour; 3. tornadoes; 4. tornadoes' paths

Page 78
Answers will vary.

Page 79
Day 1: 2. full of cheer; 3. full of pain; 4. full of use; circle purple, red, blue; **Day 2:** 2. full of joy; 3. full of fear; 4. full of color; circle popcorn, carrot, bread; **Day 3:** 2. one who sells; 3. one who bowls; 4. one who drives; circle deer, lion, dog; **Day 4:** 2. one who serves; 3. one who dives; 4. one who bakes; circle nose, leg, arm

Page 80
1. ful; 2. ful; 3. er; 4. er; 5. er; 6. ful; 7. ful; 8. er; Clothes—shirt, pants, shorts, socks, hat; Food—beans, salad, rice, meat, yogurt

Page 81
Days 1, 2, 3, 4: Answers will vary.

Page 82
1.–3. Answers will vary.

Page 83
Day 1: 1. ship; 2. dish; 3. shin; plate/dish, damp/wet, ship/boat; **Day 2:** 1. chip; 2. chop; 3. chin; paste/glue, wish/hope, like/enjoy; **Day 3:** 1. this; 2. with; 3. thin; pal/friend, cool/chilly, taxi/cab; **Day 4:** 1. white; 2. when; 3. whirl; smile/grin, laugh/giggle, unhappy/sad

Page 84
1. beach; 2. seashells; 3. that; 4. When; 5. children; 6. women; 7. loud; 8. middle; 9. nice; 10. start; 11. Answers will vary.

Page 85
Day 1: 1. his clothes; 2. on the desk; 3. plate of old food; 4. time to do chores; **Day 2:** 1. angry; 2. He thought they were not fun; 3. play outside; 4. his friends; **Day 3:** 1. told his friends that he was going to clean his room; 2. clean his room; 3. every week; 4. takes out the trash and walks the dog; **Day 4:** 1. his friends talking to his mom; 2. that they did chores; 3. a to-do list; 4. make his bed, pick up his clothes, throw out the old food, and move the shoes

Page 86
1.–4. Answers will vary.

Page 87
Day 1: 1. Mariah wants to get a new pet.; 2. Her Aunt Lisa does not want a cat or dog.; 3. Maybe they can get a fish.; 4. Fish are easy to take care of.; **Day 2:** 1. Shane likes it when it rains.; 2. He puts on his big rain boots.; 3. Then, he jumps in the puddles.; 4. He forgets his umbrella all the time.; **Day 3:** 1. Casey loves to color with pencils.; 2. She makes her drawings colorful.; 3. She will color for more than an hour.; 4. Her mom likes to display the drawings.; **Day 4:** 1. Jorge did not feel well at school.; 2. He went to the nurse's office to rest.; 3. The nurse called his dad at his job.; 4. His dad will come pick him up.

Page 88
Dear Mrs. Huber,
You are my favorite teacher! I am glad I had you this year. I will miss you this summer. I will come back to visit you when school starts.
I learned a lot in your class. You are kind and nice. I hope you have a fun summer!
Love,
Jayla

CD-104596 • © Carson-Dellosa